*Fourth Edition*

# History and Historians

## A Historiographical Introduction

Mark T. Gilderhus

*Texas Christian University*

Prentice Hall
Upper Saddle River, NJ 07458

**Library of Congress Cataloging-in-Publication Data**

Gilderhus, Mark T.
   History and historians : a historiographical introduction / Mark
T. Gilderhus.--4th ed.
      p.   cm
   Includes bibliographical references and index.
   ISBN 0-13-011582-7
   1. History--Philosophy.   2. Historiography.   3. History--
Methodology.      I. Title.
   D16.8.G533   2000
   901--dc21                                                    99-19083
                                                                      CIP


Editorial/Production Supervision and Design: *Harriet Tellem*
Executive Editor: *Todd R. Armstrong*
Prepress and Manufacturing Buyer: *Lynn Pearlman*
Editorial Assistant: *Holly Jo Brown*
Art Director: *Jayne Conte*

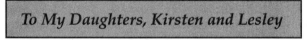

*To My Daughters, Kirsten and Lesley*

This book was set in 10/12 Palatino by Lynn Pearlman and was printed
and bound by Courier, Westford. The cover was printed by Phoenix Color
Corporation.

© 2000, 1996, 1992, 1987 by Prentice-Hall, Inc.
Pearson Education
Upper Saddle River, NJ 07458

Printed in the United States of America
10   9   8   7   6   5   4   3   2

ISBN  0-13-011582-7

Prentice-Hall International (UK) Limited, *London*
Prentice-Hall of Australia Pty. Limited, *Sydney*
Prentice-Hall Canada, Inc., *Toronto*
Prentice-Hall Hispanoamericana, S.A., *Mexico*
Prentice-Hall of India Private Limited, *New Delhi*
Prentice-Hall of Japan, Inc., *Tokyo*
Pearson Education PLC, *Asia*
Editora Prentice-Hall do Brasil, Ltda., *Rio de Janeiro*

# Contents

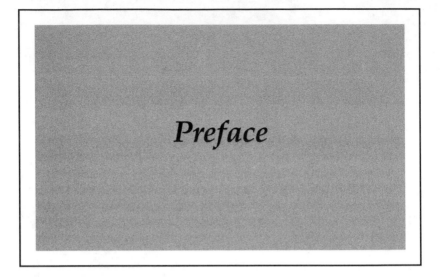

# Preface

This book provides a brief survey of Western historical thinking from ancient times to the present and also an introduction to some of the main issues and problems in historiography, philosophy of history, and historical method. It seeks to strike a balanced coverage and to make such concerns accessible to beginning students. Novice historians need to encounter questions of theory in order to grasp the nature of the discipline, but many probably lack the prerequisites to take on R. G. Collingwood straight. This small work may ease the transition.

I want to express my thanks to former colleagues who shared some of these interests, notably George M. Dennison, president of the University of Montana, and Professors Harry Rosenberg, Manfred J. Enssle, Thomas J. Knight, and James E. Hansen III of the history department at Colorado State University. Steve Dalphin, formerly of Prentice Hall, played an important role in moving the first edition toward publication. D. Clayton Brown, my department chair at Texas Christian University, aided in the process of putting together this fourth edition by providing support and encouragement. I would also like to thank Loretta Burns of Mankato State University for reviewing the manuscript for this new edition.

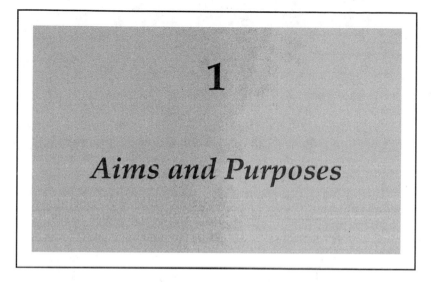

# 1

# *Aims and Purposes*

Why bother with the study of history? What possible connections exist between an increasingly remote past and our own predicaments in the present? Can stories about other peoples in other places and other times have any meaning in an age of vaulting technology and traumatizing change? Is it reasonable to think that anyone can benefit from the experiences of others in presumably unprecedented and perilous times? These questions hold more than rhetorical importance and require serious answers. College and university students in all programs of study need to know what they can hope to learn and how their educational experiences will affect their capacity to think and act creatively in the future.

Skeptics have often argued that a knowledge of history will not provide much help. American industrialist Henry Ford characterized history as "bunk." Although the observation probably tells more about the limitations of Ford's mind than about the nature of history, other luminaries have expressed similar reservations. In the seventeenth century, French scientist and mathematician René Descartes worried that undue curiosity about the past would result in excessive ignorance of the present. Another Frenchman, François Marie Arouet de Voltaire, a philosopher and historian, described history as "a pack of tricks we play on the dead." Although he intended his comment as an appeal for more accurately written history, if misunderstood it could support the skeptics who put down historians by dividing them into three camps: those who lie, those who are mistaken, and those who do not know. Even so powerful a thinker as Georg Wilhelm Friedrich Hegel, a nineteenth-century German, feared that the only thing we can learn from history is that no one learns anything from history.

Recently, more optimistic commentators have expressed greater faith. In the summer of 1989, for example, Francis Fukuyama, a State Department planner and a Harvard-trained expert on the former Soviet Union, created a stir in political and academic circles by arguing that the termination of the Cold War really constituted "the end of history." Drawing upon a kind of "philosophy of history" as a means of comprehending the significance of contemporary events, Fukuyama stated that "there is some larger process at work...that gives coherence and order to the daily headlines." For the twentieth century, he characterized the process as "a paroxysm of ideological violence" in the developed world, pitting the values of Western liberalism first against "the remnants of absolutism, then bolshevism and fascism, and finally an updated Marxism that threatened to lead to the ultimate apocalypse of nuclear war." But now the end had come, culminating in "The triumph of the West, of the Western *idea.*" According to Fukuyama, "What we may be witnessing is not just the end of the Cold War, or the passing of a particular period of postwar history, but the end point of mankind's ideological evolution and the universalization of Western liberal democracy as the final form of human government." This grandiose, provocative, and controversial affirmation elicited diverse responses from enthusiasts and critics. During the subsequent decade of the 1990s, the magnitude of racial, ethnic, and religious conflict, often violent, sometimes genocidal, raised serious doubts. Nevertheless, Fukuyama properly suggests that observers of and participants in the events of the present day will have trouble understanding much about their world unless they possess a solid grasp of history.[1]

A similar point emerged early in 1991 from a discussion of "The Uses of History" by Albert Shanker, the president of the American Federation of Teachers. Pointing specifically to the debate in the U.S. Congress over the question of whether to wage war against Iraq in the Persian Gulf, Shanker noted that the speakers filled their arguments and counterarguments with references to history:

Members talked about Socrates and Abraham Lincoln; the Mexican-American War and the Peloponnesian war…They cited St. Augustine and St. Thomas Aquinas, James Madison and Winston Churchill. Some talked about the appeasement of Hitler at Munich and Mussolini in Ethiopia; others about the Tonkin Gulf resolution that led to our deep entanglement in the Vietnam War.

According to Shanker, they did so not simply as "a way of fancying up their speeches…in a Congressional version of Trivial Pursuit" but rather "to help them think about and explain the decision they were making—to each other and to the American people." Different delegates drew different conclusions, but they all used history as "a tool…to reason and think about the crisis …to frame the debate…to make clear exactly where they stood." Shanker observed that, "No one could have followed the debates or had an intelligent opinion about the wisest course of action …without at least a basic knowledge of history." For this reason, he assigned a large measure of public significance to the discipline.[2] A plausible line of speculation suggests that United States General H. Norman Schwarzkopf in his conduct of the war benefited considerably from his study of military history. Without it he might not have been able to think of ways to defeat his enemy at minimum cost through the use of a vast flanking movement, referred to in some circles as "Schlieffen Plan Left," a successful approximation of the German move against France in 1914.

Undoubtedly the study and writing of history can become a serious and risky endeavor. While faced with large and daunting responsibilities in their work, historians must confront their intellectual shortcomings, their incomprehension of the workings of the world, and their limited capacity to interpret their evidence, almost always messy, incomplete, and susceptible to different forms of understanding. As humble practitioners, they should look upon their findings as tentative, subject in most cases to revision or rejection in the future. At the same time, they should take joy in the quest, confidant that on occasion they fulfill useful and important functions.

Most historians regard the study of history as a way for human beings to acquire self-knowledge. Edward Gibbon, the great English historian of the Roman Empire, sadly described the historical record as consisting of "the crimes, follies, and misfortunes of mankind." Though certainly indicative of a wretched and dismal state of affairs, his remark also held forth the possibility of escaping from such conditions through rational inquiry. Transcendence over the past could come about only through knowledge.

Other historians have invoked their discipline as a kind of ethical sanction. Lord Acton, a Victorian Englishman and a devout Roman Catholic, insisted on maintaining "morality as the sole impartial criterion of men and things." He called upon historians to act as arbiters, defending the proper standards, out of an expectation perhaps that the threat of disapproval in the future might discourage incorrect behavior in the present. Historians should hold malefactors accountable for their misdeeds. Tacitus, a historian of the Roman empire, took such an approach, and in all likelihood others will do the same with Richard M. Nixon and Bill Clinton.

Sometimes historians have presumed the existence of links between the past and the future, suggesting that comprehension of what has taken place might well prepare people for what will come about. How to get ready for the unknown has always been a problem. George Santayana, a Harvard philosopher, asserted early in the twentieth century that people who forget about the past are condemned to repeat it. This utilitarian conception saw in the discipline a way of developing workable strategies for survival. History comprised the recollections of all people. Santayana's belief affirmed that lessons learned from experience could aid in the avoidance of mistakes, pitfalls, and catastrophes in the future.

As a body of knowledge, history has a long and honorable tradition in Western civilization. Although definitions and points of emphasis have changed from time to time, the written narratives have always centered on human affairs and purportedly set forth truths. This latter statement means merely that historians have some good reason in the form of evidence for believing in the validity of their accounts. Contemporary American historian Paul Conkin has provided a succinct description. A history "is a true story about the human past."[3] Obviously the adjectives "true" and "human" are crucial. The quality of "truth" distinguishes history from legend, fable, and myth, which admittedly may be "true" in some ways but usually not literally. The concern for the human past requires that historians pay attention to the events in nature primarily when they affect the activities of people. Volcanic eruptions, for example, hold an interest mainly when they bury cities such as Pompeii.

From ancient times to the present, all peoples have told stories about themselves, their ancestors, and their origins. The Assyrians carved into stone monuments the names and deeds of their kings for everyone to see. The inscriptions also contained warnings, indeed, curses threatening to punish transgressors who might deface the artifacts and violate the integrity of the record. The earliest tales usually dwelt upon extraordinary occurrences characterized as unusual, wonderful, fabulous, terrible, or miraculous. They told of spectacular events, often featuring displays of supernatural power in which the gods and the goddesses participated in human affairs and sometimes determined the outcomes. In the present day, such renditions confuse us because, by our standards, they seem to mingle the true with the untrue and the believable with the unbelievable. However, they are not necessarily evidence of overwrought imaginations or low intelligence in ancient times. Rather, they bear out the historians' truism that different peoples in different times and places literally saw and experienced the world differently. It may also be that very divergent conceptions of truth and believability have separated the present from the past.

A view of history more consistent with our own developed in the ancient world when iconoclasts announced their disbelief in traditional, oral accounts and insisted on setting the record straight. In Greece, early in the fifth century B.C., Herodotus of Halicarnassus composed some of the first "critical history" in the Western tradition by writing "the truth" about the Greek wars against the Persians. In putting together *The Histories*, Herodotus employed verifiable information, using eyewitness accounts, some official records of state, and his own observations. To his admirers, he was "the father of history." Ever since Herodotus, historians have tried to tell true stories about the human past.

For two-and-one-half millennia, the study of history has satisfied many aims and purposes. In all likelihood, various students of the subject first acquired an interest out of simple fascination. As curious and inquisitive beings, they enjoyed the sheer fun of vicarious experience while asking, "What was it like?" Through the exercise of imagination, they could take part in many things, such as the Punic Wars or the Renaissance. Some reveled in the possession of odd and esoteric pieces of information, possibly the kind of armaments used in battle during the Hundred Years' War or the lineage of Swedish kings, while others found in history a source of instruction, that is, a way of making the course of human affairs intelligible, or at least some portions thereof. As noted by a European folk saying, people are not lost until they don't know where they have been. Historians seek to keep us from getting lost by locating us in time and figuring out where we have been.

Although simple curiosity is a sound reason for embarking upon historical studies, professional scholars usually bring additional incentives to their work. Many are impelled by a strong sense of psychological necessity to make things intelligible, a consideration that undoubtedly operates in most other areas of intellectual endeavor. Scholars want to bring some measure of order and predictability to the world. They dislike disorder and unpredictability because random and haphazard events defy comprehension and entail danger. Such vulnerability implies futility and the possibility of extinction. Scholars want to know what is likely to happen under various sets of circumstances. Most academic disciplines strive to make accurate predictions about probable outcomes. Such is the case in physics, chemistry, sociology, and political science. It is also true in history, except that in this discipline the process takes place backward in time instead of forward. On the basis of fragmentary and imperfect evidence, historians make retroactive predictions, that is, retrodictions, about what probably happened in the past and, in so doing, seek to define cause-and-effect relationships to make the flow of events understandable. Whenever historians make cause-and-effect statements—for example, "Americans moved west because of the Panic of 1837"—they affirm their belief in the intelligibility of events in the human world. Things happen for reasons, and inquiring minds can grasp them.

Such assumptions are deeply engrained in the traditions of Western civilization. Whether they are actually true is perhaps less important than the historians' conviction that they should be. For historians, the identification of cause-and-effect relationships establishes meaning and comprehensibility but can never be proven as literally true. They have to be taken on a large measure of faith. As an example of an alternate view, Kurt Vonnegut's novel *Slaughterhouse Five* contains an intriguing vignette. The central character, the remarkable Billy Pilgrim, has the capacity to move around in time and space. He can travel into the past, into the future, and also beyond the confines of Earth. In one episode, he is kidnapped by extraterrestrial beings from the planet Tralfamador. They put Billy Pilgrim on public display, locked up in a transparent geodesic dome with another captive, Montana Wildhack, a voluptuous movie starlet. The Tralfamadorans enjoy watching the two cavort about and also engage them in philosophical discussions. Billy Pilgrim amuses and awes his captors by affirming his belief that cause-and-effect relationships govern the course of events. Things happen because other things make them happen. The Tralfamadorans have a different notion. For them, things happen merely because they happen—randomly, haphazardly, inexplicably, chaotically. The adoption of any such worldview would make the work of historians next to impossible.

History also provides a way to study the identity of people, both individually and collectively. In some ways, this function of history parallels psychiatry and psychoanalysis in that these fields also endeavor to clarify human behavior in the present by making knowledge of the past both conscious and explicit. Just as psychiatrists and psychoanalysts seek to treat aberrant or disturbed conduct by scrutinizing repressed or unconscious memories, so historians try to arrive at a fuller understanding of the actions of people by examining their history. Robin G. Collingwood, a British philosopher and historian, liked to suggest that human beings possess no nature; they have merely history. As malleable creatures, they become whatever their experiences make of them.

Even allowing for some exaggeration, Collingwood has a compelling point. Historical experience shapes and molds the identity of people in important ways. Most of us recognize this claim as a fact in our rituals. For centuries, Jewish people in their Passover feasts have told the story of ancient Israel and the special covenant with Yahweh, their God, and have managed, in spite of isolation and dispersion, to maintain a collective sense of group identity. In a less profound way, Fourth of July ceremonies in the United States serve a similar purpose. By invoking patriotic lore about the American Revolution, the people of the country establish a sense of solidarity by celebrating the origins of their nation. Just as a single person might explore the question "Who am I?" by thinking through life experiences, historians tell the life stories of peoples and groups. When we ask, "Who are the Kurds?" or "the Germans?" or "the Taiwanese?" or "Who are we?" the narratives of history provide one place to begin.

Another reason for studying history is utilitarian and practical. According to this rationale, history has a useful application because it helps us better to calculate the anticipated consequences of our own acts. George Santayana probably had this idea in mind when he said that people will repeat the past if they forget it. His words should not be taken too literally. The Second World War will not happen again, even if we neglect to read and write about it. Santayana meant something deeper. He knew that history is the collective memory of humankind and that the onset of a mass amnesia would have bad effects. For one thing, it would prevent the young from learning from the old. Each generation would have to find fire and invent the wheel over and over again. Without memory, we would have trouble functioning and making do in the world. What each generation transmits to the next can be understood in some measure as lessons in the art of survival.

Philosopher Karl R. Popper pointed out another facet of the problem. He believed that, above all, social scientists and historians should contemplate the unintended consequences of deliberate human acts. Sometimes things go wrong. Historical actors set out to accomplish a set of goals and actually bring about unanticipated or contrary results. Popper wanted students of human affairs to investigate the linkages between intentions and outcomes. Napoleon's attempt to dominate Europe destroyed feudal structures and cleared the way for modernization. In South Vietnam, the United States employed military force, supposedly in defense of the right of self-determination, and facilitated the obliteration of a small country. Such ironies, sometimes tragic, sometimes comic, abound in human experience. Theologian, philosopher, and historian Reinhold Niebuhr pondered this maddening issue in his book *The Irony of American History* and warned that the actual consequences of our acts sometimes subvert our commitments to high ideals. We need to be careful in pursuing grandiose purposes because so often they go awry. If we could better reckon the relationship between aims and outcomes, we would vastly improve our chances of behaving more creatively in the world.

Historians typically construct their narratives by affirming the existence of cause-and-effect relationships and appraising the connections between the actions of historical figures, their presumed motives, and the actual consequences. The following three-stage model has merely descriptive, not prescriptive, intent. It shows how many historians do carry out their work but sets forth no requirement that they must proceed in this fashion.

During the first step, historians begin their inquiry by asking, "What happened? How did the historical actors behave? What did they do?" This part is the easiest. As long as some kinds of artifacts exist, possibly oral traditions, stone tablets, manuscripts, diaries, newspaper accounts, or official records of state, historians can arrive at some determinations. If no remnants of the past exist at all, then no written history is possible.

During the second step, historians must account for the actors' behavior by asking the question, "Why?" The answer usually calls for an explanation or interpretation and has tricky implications because it entails an assortment of methodological and theoretical dangers. Historians traditionally have employed a "rational human" model of behavior in framing their explanations. They have assumed that most people set rational goals for themselves and then seek to achieve them through the exercise of reason and logic. In more recent times, dissenters have criticized this approach as hopelessly antiquated. Marxist scholars, for example, have argued that economic and class relationships usually determine behavior, no matter what the pretext, and that ostensibly principled and righteous actions often emanate from hidden purposes aimed at self-aggrandizement. Similarly, the advocates of psychohistory have rejected the "rational human" model. In their efforts to apply psychoanalytical theories to history, they find the wellspring of human behavior not in reason and logic but in repressed impulses tucked away deep within the recesses of the psyche. Such disparities of understanding mean that discussions of motive are always tentative and uncertain.

In the final step, many historians try to evaluate the consequences of events. How did things turn out, for good or for ill? Who benefited and who suffered? Did the outcome make the effort worthwhile? On such big and significant questions, historians seldom agree. The reason is obvious. Any attempt to address them will draw upon differing and rival value systems— that is, divergent standards of judgment—and no means exist by which to reconcile them. How can historians accurately measure the costs and gains of the Mexican Revolution after 1910? About one million people died out of a population of twelve million. If the great rebellion had never occurred, would "natural progress" have made Mexico a better place at less expense? No scholar has any good way of knowing for sure. Was the Second World War really "the good war," and was the use of atomic bombs necessary? Among other things, history involves the practitioners in an ongoing and sometimes unresolvable debate over the meaning of human experiences.

Historians practice their craft in a kind of intellectual minefield in which all sorts of unknown and unanticipated dangers pose threats, and the best of projects can blow up before them. The evidence often is too sparse to tell the whole story. Even when it exists in abundance, the difficulties of explanation, interpretation, and evaluation are immense. Yet, historians persist in their toil, seeking to render some small portions of human experience intelligible. This book is intended as an introduction to the practices and patterns of historical thinking.

## RECOMMENDED READINGS

Engaging observations and pungent definitions of the nature of history appear in Ferenc M. Szasz, "The Many Meanings of History," *The History Teacher*, 7 (Aug. 1974), 552–63; 7 (Nov. 1974), 54–63: 8 (Feb. 1975), 208–16; and another piece provided by subscribers, 9 (Feb. 1976), 217–27. Introductory works considering aims and purposes include Fritz Stern, ed., *The Varieties of History: From Voltaire to the Present* (New York: William Collins Publishers, 1956); Allan J. Lichtman and Valerie French, *Historians and the Living Past: The Theory and Practice of Historical Study* (Arlington Heights, IL: AHM Publishing, 1978); Carl G. Gustavson, *The Mansion of History* (New York: McGraw-Hill, 1976); and Arthur Marwick, *The Nature of History* (New York: Dell Publishing, 1970). R. G. Collingwood, *The Idea of History* (New York: Oxford University Press, 1956), although difficult for beginners, is indispensable. Karl R. Popper's discussion of "Prediction and Prophecy in the Social Sciences" appears in the collection edited by Patrick Gardiner, *Theories of History* (New York: The Free Press, 1959), 276–85.

## ENDNOTES

1.  Francis Fukuyama, "The End of History," *The National Interest* (Summer 1989), 2–18; *idem, The End of History and the Last Man* (New York: Free Press, 1992). An attack on Fukuyama's views appears in Keith

Windschuttle, *The Killing of History: How a Discipline Is Being Murdered by Literary Critics and Social Theorists* (Paddington, Australia: Macleay Press, 1996), 159–73.

2. Albert Shanker, "Where We Stand, Debating War in the Persian Gulf and the Uses of History," *The New Republic* (February 1991), 7.

3. Paul K. Conkin and Roland N. Stromberg, *The Heritage and Challenge of History* (New York: Dodd, Mead and Company, 1971), 131.

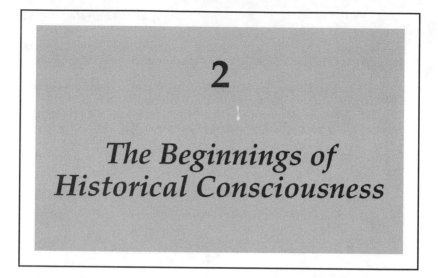

# 2

# *The Beginnings of Historical Consciousness*

The traditions of Western civilization possess a distinctive level of historical consciousness. This awareness developed in large measure from the legacies of the Jews, the Greeks, and the early Christians. The Jews and later the Christians imposed upon the events of the past a sense of meaning, structure, and process. For them, the past merged with the present and the future and moved inexorably toward a set of definite and knowable goals. The Greeks, meanwhile, contributed an insistence upon studying the past critically and scientifically to determine the truth. For them, the distinction between history and mythology became fundamental.

In contrast, the earliest human beings had little historical consciousness. They lived in an expansive present in which the urgencies of mere survival pressed incessantly upon them. Indeed, the terrors of the past—the recollection of impermanence, hunger, death, catastrophe, and destruction—may have created psychological barriers against the act of remembering. The trauma of mere existence removed all meaning from past events, except perhaps the negative connotations. To whatever extent the earliest people conceived of a time dimension, their impressions took on a cyclical form—that is, a conception of events moving more or less pointlessly in a circle. Things occurred, went away, and then recurred, much in the fashion of days, nights, and seasons. For ancient peoples, the familiar and predictable patterns of nature became a way of organizing the unfamiliar and unpredictable happenings in the human world.

Religious myths, legends, and fables satisfied the need of ancient peoples to know about their origins and predecessors. These tales often posited the existence of a "golden age" during which the people lived harmoniously among themselves and with nature. The story in the book of *Genesis* about Adam and Eve in the Garden of Eden is an example. Other accounts presumed a close relationship with supernatural beings in which the gods and goddesses often possessed humanlike characteristics and achieved their purposes through the manipulation and control of the lesser beings. In Greek mythology, the gods competed with one another for love and power, waged war on one another, and sometimes failed. Infallibility was not necessarily an attribute of supernatural beings in the ancient world. The deities also had a capacity for cruelty when they sought vengeance and inflicted retribution. When disasters and cataclysms took place, ancient people normally attributed them to the will of the supernatural powers. The Greek notion of hubris, meaning self-destructive pride, required that the gods bring down mere mortals who overreached themselves. In all likelihood, such myths and legends also had political importance. By affirming a connection with the divinities through lineage or proximity, ancient rulers could legitimize their right to govern.

Some ancient peoples kept no records and hence have no recoverable history. Others, such as the Egyptians, Sumerians, Assyrians, and Hittites, left written artifacts dating from the third and second millennia B.C. Many of these consisted of lists and inscriptions recounting the deeds of great men. They testified to the emergence of a primitive historical consciousness, perhaps a sense of chronology, but showed little appreciation for the effect of one event upon another or the interrelationships among them. Instead, these registers presented bits of information in isolation from others. Sometimes they recited the major accomplishments or occurrences during the reign of a king, noting the year the wall was built or the temple completed, the time of the great famine or plague, or when enemies laid waste to the city. Accounts of warfare figured prominently. Graphic, brutal, even sadistic, descriptions reported terrible punishments visited upon conquered foes. An Assyrian document reported these acts performed by a king named Assurnâsirpal:

600 of their warriors I put to the sword; 3,000 captives I burned with fire; I did not leave a single one of them alive to serve as a hostage...Hulai, their governor, I flayed and his skin I spread upon the wall of the city; the city I destroyed, I devastated, I burned with fire.[1]

In another episode, the same monarch cut off the hands, noses, and ears of another set of adversaries, put out their eyes, and removed their heads, from which he constructed a pillar. Such documents contained the raw material of history but did not in themselves constitute history. They provided no interpretations or analyses. They reported victories in battle but not the means of winning. The blood lust exhibited in them suggests why the horror of recollecting the past might have repelled ancient peoples.

The Jews of ancient Israel developed a very different outlook. For them, history became more important than for any other ancient people. Indeed, it became a kind of obsession, the comprehension of which established the meaning of their existence and affirmed their own unique sense of destiny. Through the processes of history, the ancient Hebrews forged a distinctive relationship with their God, Yahweh. He had chosen them as a special people with particular obligations and responsibilities. The experience of deliverance from bondage in Egypt into the Promised Land became a memory seared upon the Jewish consciousness. In return, they had a commitment to comport themselves according to the Law. By their conception of the Covenant, the Jewish people would enjoy peace and plenty as long as they complied with the divine will. In contrast, calamity, suffering, and woe would descend upon them if they violated the Ten Commandments. The Jews saw the hand of God in human affairs. He rewarded good and faithful behavior and punished transgressions. The Jews reported their history accordingly in the books of the Old Testament.

Hebrew historical writing was more the product of religious experience and faith than a manifestation of critical or rational inquiry. The Jews interpreted the events in the lives of their people according to intense convictions. Bias and inconsistency, to be sure, crept into their narratives. For example, Jewish writers sometimes incorporated different versions of the same events from diverse oral traditions. Nevertheless, they also displayed a capacity for hardheaded objectivity. A remarkable passage in the second book of Samuel describes the antics of King David at a festival, "leaping and dancing" about, even uncovering himself before the handmaidens of his servants. Much disturbed by the scene, Michal, the daughter of Saul, felt disdain for David and later, upon encountering him, remarked ironically, "How glorious was the king of Israel today." As observed by Michael Grant, a historian of the ancient world, "David does not show up very brilliantly there."[2] In spite of his heroic stature, he was depicted unidealistically. The Jews knew how to exercise some measure of detachment.

The Greeks contributed something of immense significance in the development of historical thought. They invented critical history as a method of sorting out the true from the false. In the classical Greek language, the term *histor* referred to a learned man who settled legal disputes. He looked into the facts and determined their accuracy through inquiry. Subsequently, as Michael Grant explained, the word *historie* meant "a search for the rational explanation and understanding of phenomena." In the fifth century B.C., two geniuses, Herodotus and Thucydides, brought about an intellectual revolution by employing such techniques and creating the writing of history.

In some ways, it is startling that such a development should have taken place in Greece, for the Greeks were not especially historically minded. To the extent that they conceived of a time dimension, they embraced a cyclical manner of thinking. Homeric poems, such as *The Iliad* and *The Odyssey*, recounted heroic, epic tales of earlier times in a grand and noble fashion, but they were not history, even though the Greeks may have thought of them as such. Rather, they consisted of legends, myths, and fables in which gods, goddesses, and heroes acted together, and supernatural forces often accounted for the progression of events. Divine wills figured prominently in human affairs. Before history could exist, a test of reason had to take place. The great accomplishments of Herodotus and Thucydides provided the model for all subsequent written history. Many modern scholars still regard the two men as ranking among the greatest historians of all time. Historiography, which is the history of historical writing, still holds them in high esteem. Indeed, new editions based on more readable translations have recently appeared, obtaining critical acclaim from scholars and indicating an ongoing interest among them in the works of Herodotus and Thucydides. These writings took the form of prose, not poetry, and allowed each author to indulge a talent in storytelling before live audiences.[3]

The Histories by Herodotus of Halicarnassus told of the Greek wars against Persia during the third decade of the fifth century B.C. The first portion provided historical background, exploring the origin of the quarrel between the two contestants. The remainder recounted the details of Persian expeditions against Greece under the kings Darius and Xerxes. Little is known about Herodotus's life. Presumably he lived about a generation after these events, and he traveled widely in order to collect material. The Persian Wars impressed him as the most important events in world history, and he made them the framework of his narrative. As he explained, he had two purposes in mind: "to preserve the memory of the past by putting on record the astonishing achievements both of our own and of the Asiatic peoples" and "to show how the two races came into conflict."[4] He achieved these aims and much more. Frequent digressions in the narrative dispensed an array of fascinating and odd bits of information, providing among other things a means of entertainment for his audience. His ethnographic and geographic accounts also suggested a broadly cultural approach. Herodotus wanted to know why the Nile flooded each year and how the Pyramids came into being. Many things piqued his curiosity, and intriguing observations followed. The Babylonians, for example, lacked medical doctors and made it a practice to put invalids in the street so they could receive advice from passersby, and the Persians made it a habit to deliberate twice on important issues, once while drunk and once while sober. The one condition served as a check on the other.

Herodotus liked to tell a good story but also employed rigorous methods. He checked his information against the reports of eyewitnesses and participants and also consulted the documents available to him—inscriptional records, archives, and official chronicles. He also departed from the custom of explaining human events as the outcome of divine will. To be sure, he never succeeded in rendering a completely secular account of history. The deities still had a role to play in human affairs. But Herodotus, more than any predecessor, interpreted the course of human affairs as the product of human wills.

Thucydides, an Athenian, wrote The Peloponnesian War, an account of the struggle between Athens and Sparta during the last three decades of the fifth century B.C. Thucydides took part in the conflict as a military commander and suffered the effects of the great plague in Athens, a horror vividly described in his writing. When forced into exile by the humiliation of a military defeat, he spent the next twenty years gathering materials for his work. Like Herodotus, he picked warfare as his subject. As he explained, he began his history "at the very outbreak of the war, in the belief that it was going to be a great war and more worth writing about than any of those which had happened in the past." He also wanted his history to be useful. Expressing a belief typical of his time, he affirmed a cyclical view in the expectation that "what happened in the past...will, in due course, tend to be repeated with some degree of similarity."[5] Thucydides intended his writing to have instructional importance as a guide to action in the future. Although history would never repeat itself exactly, he anticipated the development of parallel circumstances and believed that the consciousness of history would bestow many benefits. All leaders should learn from the mistakes of the past. Indeed, they could master the arts of politics, statecraft, and warfare only from the study of history.

Thucydides was scrupulous in his methods. As a careful student of causation, he took pains to identify the process by which the Peloponnesian War came about. His analysis attributed the war's real or underlying reason to Sparta's fear of Athens's growing power. He also paid heed to individual motives but used a convention sometimes troublesome for modern scholars. Following the practices of Greek drama and Herodotus, Thucydides had historical figures deliver speeches in which they revealed their aims and intentions. Critics have attacked the use of such monologues as false. Even if the historian had heard them, how could he remember the details? Apologists, in contrast, have pointed out that while not literally true, such devices enabled Thucydides to elucidate his understanding of the actors' characters and goals. In a sense, Thucydides had them say what their nature and the situation called for.

Thucydides, more than Herodotus, explained events in secular terms. In *The Peloponnesian War*, things happened not because the gods willed them but because of human activities. People had to endure the consequences of their own acts. Thucydides also strove for objectivity. His detachment and single-minded determination to stick to the essentials of the story made for less entertainment than in Herodotus. No amusing digressions provided diversions for the listener or the reader. But the undoubted brilliance of his work inspired David Hume many centuries later to write, "The first page of Thucydides is the beginning of all true history."[6]

The quality of Greek historical writing declined after Herodotus and Thucydides. Much also became lost to posterity. Nevertheless, the two masters exerted strong influence over their progeny. In the second century b.c., Polybius, a Greek, embraced them as his models. He insisted that a historian must travel to see the sites, participate in public events, and utilize the documentary records. He must also have a grand theme. Polybius's *Universal History* told of Rome's expansion over the whole of the Mediterranean world. He also intended that his work have useful effects. As a form of practical instruction, it should equip serious readers better to act upon the future. Polybius passed on to the Romans the best of the Greek traditions in historical writing.

The Romans, strongly affected by the Greeks, also concentrated their attention on the political and military activities of the ruling elites. But, unlike the Greeks, they were less concerned with detachment and objectivity. As serious moralists, they preferred to pass judgments and to depict that which was corrupt or exemplary. Late in the first century b.c., for example, Sallust wrote from an outsider's point of view about the affairs of state, taking the leaders to task for their mistakes and misdeeds and warning of the effects of decadence and decay. Titus Livy reported on the reign of Augustus, a period of forty-five years during which peace returned after an era of conflict and civil war. His *History of Rome* comprised an astounding 142 volumes and emphasized the role of civic virtue in the expansion of the Roman Republic. Unlike the historians who were also men of action, notably Thucydides, Titus Livy never held a public office, instead devoting his whole life to research and writing. The Romans also developed an interest in biography, emphasizing the role of personal character. Among the most famous biographers, Plutarch, writing in Greek, studied the roles of soldiers and statesmen, and Suetonius composed the *Lives of the Caesars.*

Two Romans, Julius Caesar and Cornelius Tacitus, had special significance. Caesar's *Commentaries* recounted firsthand his military exploits against the Gauls, Germans, and Britons in the middle of the first century b.c. This unique and original work, spare and unadorned, established a stylistic model of Latin prose and also a new literary genre. As the memoirs of a field commander, Caesar's writings showed less interest in character and personality than in action. As a result, future scholars obtained more information about the Gallic War than any other military operation in the ancient world. Caesar also wrote with an eye toward his reputation before the governing classes in Rome and before posterity. Political and military memoirs are seldom self-effacing.

Tacitus, Rome's greatest historian, produced several works on political and military subjects. The most notable, *The Annals of Imperial Rome*, described the affairs of the empire from the beginning of Tiberius's reign in A.D. 14 until the year 68, soon after the death of Nero. Written early in the second century A.D., the book vividly depicted personalities and also the corruption and degeneracy of Rome's rulers. Typical of Roman historians, Tacitus, formerly a state official, commended public virtue and condemned immorality and evil, especially the excesses of the emperors and the self-serving cliques around them. He called them to account, often with sardonic irony and deep pessimism. Tacitus put little faith in the redemptive capabilities of human nature. For him, Rome, the center of the world, had gone into eclipse. His themes centered on the growth of political tyranny and the decline of Roman virtue. While employing the traditional format, a narration of events year by year, he emphasized the dangers of concentrating political power in one man, always a hazardous practice because it allows individual character flaws to inflict maximum damage. Tacitus's tales of wrongdoing in the struggle for personal advancement featured adultery, incest, murder, matricide, patricide, and infanticide. He shared with Lord Acton a view expressed some eighteen centuries later, holding that "power tends to corrupt, and absolute power corrupts absolutely." The careers of the debauched Tiberius and the brutal Nero provided cases in point.

Meanwhile, an emerging Christian view of history took on more cosmopolitan forms, extending beyond the provincial and self-centered fixations of Greece and Rome. It developed slowly during several centuries and out of harsh experience. The earliest Christians had little historical consciousness. They conceived of themselves as living in a small, closed universe, very near the termination of time. Because the end of the world and the Second Coming of Christ dominated their expectations, their anticipations of the future held more significance than their perceptions of the past. Later, when they had to face up to the fact that their religious prophecies had not come about, they could not avoid a confrontation with historical problems.

For one reason, when Christian missionaries sought converts in the world of the Gentiles, they needed to establish the authority of revealed religion based on its historicity. From various sources, such as oral traditions and the like, they compiled the Gospels, consisting of stories about the life and sayings of Jesus and his ministry, crucifixion, and resurrection. The Christian insistence that such occurrences actually had taken place grounded their beliefs in an interpretation of historical experience and affirmed the veracity of their claims before believers. History also became important when the early Christians tried to devise proper connections with the Old Testament. The identification of Jesus with the Messiah of Hebrew prophecy necessarily engaged them with the teachings of the Hebrew prophets. Once the early Christians came to regard the Old Testament as Holy Scripture, they also formulated an explanation of the relationship between the past, the present, and the future. Ultimately they conceived of the whole of the Old Testament as an anticipation of Jesus Christ and a preparation for him. For them, such prophecies became an important means by which to ascertain the designs of Divine Providence.

Christianity later took on some of the attributes of universal history through its efforts to appeal to pagans. To obtain prestige within the Roman Empire, again arguing on the basis of history, Christians tried to show that Hebrew wisdom had roots more ancient than Greek philosophy. Moses after all lived a long time before Plato. Other attempts to link the experiences of Jews and Gentiles compelled Christians to develop ideas about the secular history of humankind. The very nature of the Scriptures, of course, contributed by starting with the Creation and then telling about the beginnings of the human race and the subsequent divisions into distinctive groups. Indeed, Christian writers of universal history followed this convention until the eighteenth and nineteenth centuries typically by beginning their narratives with creation accounts based on their understanding of the book of *Genesis*.

Christians within the Roman Empire suffered the effects of oppression and persecution for their beliefs but finally obtained a great triumph when the Emperor Constantine converted to their religion early in the fourth century. This outcome encouraged the writing of ecclesiastical history, detailing the rise of Christianity throughout the Mediterranean world. Eusebius of Caesarea in Syria Palestine was an early practitioner. His *History of the Church* and other works demonstrated how all previous history, especially the Hebrew experience, had led to the Christian revelation. Eusebius took pains to rebut the pagan charge that the newly invented Christian religion appealed only to ignorant people. Quite the contrary, he argued, the traditions stretched backward in time into a glorious past far beyond the Greeks. His work celebrated the Christian victory in taking possession of Rome.

A century later under very different circumstances, St. Augustine, the bishop of Hippo in North Africa, wrote *The City of God*, the most influential statement of a Christian interpretation of history ever devised. Augustine's work followed in response to a catastrophe in the year 410, when Alaric and the Goths captured the city of Rome for three days of looting, pillage, and rape. This horrifying event, verging on the unimaginable, ignited fears of resurgent barbarism overwhelming Roman civilization and also provoked pagan charges of Christian responsibility. Adherents of the new religion supposedly had led the people away from the ancient Roman gods, who in this way had taken retribution upon the Eternal City for its neglect. Augustine in reply wrote his powerful work between the years 413 and 426. To an extent, he labored as a partisan and polemicist in defense of the Christians. In the first ten chapters, he absolved them of the blame, showing that equivalent disasters had occurred before, even when the inhabitants worshiped pagan gods. In the remaining ten chapters, he developed a new and unique approach to universal history. Drawing upon earlier Jewish and Christian writings, he developed an analysis that would dominate European thinking for over a thousand years.

As an organizing principle, Augustine established a dualism distinguishing fundamentally between the profane and the sacred. He referred to the former as the earthly "city of man" and to the latter as the heavenly "city of God." Though intermingled on Earth for the remainder of time, the two communities took on distinctively different characteristics. The first, the secular city, featured self-love and an absorption with the ways of the flesh. The second, the Eternal City, affirmed spiritual love for God above all things. Although Augustine traced the progress of both cities until his own time, his main preoccupation centered on sacred history, that is, his attempt to elucidate the ways of God toward his creation and to establish the appropriate correlations of human events with Biblical accounts.

Augustine's work also held important implications for the philosophy of history. His sense of time, derived from Hebrew conceptions, rejected outright the Greek idea of cyclical movements. For Augustine, endless revolvings and pointless repetitions would have rendered history meaningless—in effect, a nullification of divine influence and purpose. Rather, he thought of history as moving along a line with a clear beginning marked by the Creation, a middle, and an end. The birth and death of Christ denoted the central events, and the salvation of all believers at the termination signified the completion of the process. The concluding triumph of the city of God over the city of man would result in the fulfillment of the final aim, the transcendence of believers beyond history into the realm of the eternal.

Augustine's conviction, endorsed in high forms of art, literature, and music by masters such as Michelangelo, Dante, and Handel, made profound imprints upon Western civilization. The schema, characterized by the two cities and the movement of events along a line, inspired Christian writers throughout the medieval period and after. They attributed prime significance to teleology and eschatology—that is, to those branches of philosophy and theology concerned with the nature of providential design and the conclusion of time during the last days. Christian predictions about the end of this world took on an Augustinian understanding of God's plan by which the Divinity sought to work out his will through history.

For over ten centuries, writers on historical subjects during the Middle Ages labored under Augustine's influence. Though Europeans during this time made distinctions between secular and sacred history, they paid the greatest attention to the latter and composed ecclesiastical or church histories, designed primarily to delineate the progress of God's work in this world. Characteristically the writing took the form of annals and chronicles, set forth by priests and monks. Such accounts became stylized, based on Augustine's model. Normally they contained a resume of universal history since the Creation, influenced often by Old Testament accounts, an affirmation of God's purpose and will, and then statements of occurrences in more recent times, showing the immanence of the divine presence in reality.

The annals, the more rudimentary form, consisted of lists in brief entry, a record of memorable events in a locality during a single year in some kind of yearbook or register. An aggregation of such entries, taken together and arranged in an annual sequence with some additional narrative, produced a chronicle. Though usually geared to record God's activities and manifestations, such sources also contained a great deal of information about secular life in Christian communities. The compilers told about the goings-on within the monastery, the deaths of bishops and kings, the outcomes of battles, and the construction of new churches. They also reported on unusual episodes, often taken as omens or portents from which to gain foretellings of the future. Eclipses and floods, the appearance of strange animals, or the birth of malformed children provided occasions for uncertainty and wonderment.

Though annals and chronicles became the main vehicles for historical writing during the medieval period, the priests and monks usually assembled their records in anonymity and hence posed a problem for modern scholars who seek to identify them. Some carried out their labors for purely personal reasons, others to keep an official record for some kind of patron, possibly by the commission of a royal court. The problem of determining authorship became even more difficult because of the prevailing practice, sometimes over several generations, of circulating the documents from one monastery to another for emendations and exchanges of information.

Although in many instances the work of several authors, the annals and chronicles bore some uniform characteristics. For example, they testified to a widespread belief in divine providence. For medieval writers, one God with paternal authority indisputably stood above humanity, watched over the course of events, and regularly influenced them through divine intervention. Such expressions of faith, of course, influenced the discussions of human behavior and the analyses of phenomena. The compilers of annals and chronicles looked upon religion as the ultimate concern of humankind and believed too that history moved teleologically according to design toward a foreordained conclusion directed by God.

Such proclivities produced a tendency toward moralistic examinations of human experience. Medieval writing often rendered verdicts and judgments, thus raising questions in the present about objectivity and truthfulness. Contemporary scholars have recognized the issue as a modern one. Most medieval chronicles would not have seen it as a problem. They looked upon an intention to tell the truth as the main responsibility. Procopius, for example, declared that "truth alone is appropriate to history," and Matthew Paris invoked an even stronger sanction against untruthful historians. "If they commit to writing that which is false, they are not acceptable to the Lord." To assure credibility, medieval writers usually informed readers of their sources of information. The following examples suggest some additional characteristics.

Procopius, a Byzantine of the sixth century, composed contemporary histories of the wars of the Emperor Justinian I against the Ostrogoths, Vandals, Visigoths, and Persians. His major work is known as the *History of the Wars*. As a writer well versed in classical Greek historiography, he embraced as his models the works of Herodotus, Thucydides, and Polybius. He also emulated their methods. He used his political connections to good advantage and managed to accompany the generals onto the battlefields. Probably he also gained access to state papers and official archives. He merits a high place within the ranks of medieval historians because of the quality and persuasiveness of his writing. Nevertheless, modern authorities concede that they have no way to test his trustworthiness, because no other sources exist against which to measure his accounts.

The Venerable Bede engaged in a very different kind of scholarship early in the eighth century. He spent most of his life in the monastery at Jarrow in Northumbria in the north of England, studying, teaching, and writing on religious, educational, and historical subjects. One of the great centers of learning in its day, the monastery of Jarrow had an excellent library. Modern scholars acclaim Bede as one of the most learned men of the early Middle Ages. His *Ecclesiastical History of the English People* is the first reliable description of early Britain, taking into account the sacred and secular aspects. Bede initially became interested in history while pondering the problem of establishing an accurate chronology of events and the proper dates for Christian festivals. Later he became intrigued with the arrival of Christianity in England, a singular and striking thing; the expansion of the Church through the country; and the effects upon the cultural and intellectual life. He discussed extensively the literary activities of monks. Though Bede seldom conducted research in the archives and repositories of the great churches and abbeys and never participated in battles, he had a high regard for valid sources and often arranged to have written accounts and other narratives brought to him from Canterbury.

In the twelfth century, Otto of Freising emerged as the greatest of the German chroniclers. Born into a noble family, a nephew of Emperor Frederick I Barbarossa, Otto became the bishop of Freising, near Salzburg in Austria, and stayed there all his life. He wrote two important works: *The Deeds of Emperor Frederick Barbarossa*, a laudatory political biography of his uncle, and the *Chronicle or History of the Two Cities*, written as a universal history and modeled on the work of St. Augustine. Otto of Freising employed a linear conception of history and presumed the existence of a beginning, the Creation, and an end, the Second Coming, after which Christians would enjoy everlasting bliss in eternity. He vividly presented the notion of the two cities and took it more literally than St. Augustine, seeing the Church actually as the representative of the Holy City. Yet, as a member of the royal family and a close observer of imperial affairs, he was more conciliatory in his attitude toward the secular state. He possessed little faith that Christianity could moderate the baser aspects of human nature in this world.

Two chroniclers of the late medieval period, Matthew Paris and Jean Froissart, also merit mention. Matthew Paris, an English monk in the thirteenth century, recorded the affairs of church and state in his own time. His *Greater Chronicle* incorporated an edited version of *Flowers of History*, the work of a predecessor, Roger of Wendover, but Matthew's narrative upon reaching the year 1236 became an independent and original source. More broadly gauged than much medieval writing, it described events in England and elsewhere, including Western Europe, the Papal states, the Latin Empire of Constantinople, the Holy Land, and even Russia. He paid special heed to politics and international intrigue but also liked to remind his readers of God's presence in this world, the role of divine providence, and the impending realities of death and last judgment. As with much medieval historical writing, according to God's plan, divine punishment almost always followed from the enactment of a sin.

In the fourteenth century, the *Chronicles* of Jean Froissart, a French priest, also centered on political and military affairs of state. He wrote with self-conscious detachment and endeavored to tell the truth in an age of chivalry. He stirringly depicted battles and heroic deeds by knights in combat. He also assumed a divine role in human affairs but worked hard to obtain accurate information. As a historian mainly concerned with the aristocracy, he took little interest in the mundane lives of the lower classes.

In summary, the historiographical traditions of the medieval period modified the Greek approach by putting supernatural powers back into history. This tendency persisted well into the modern era. By the fourteenth century, such writings had become formalistic and repetitive. Medieval chroniclers typically concentrated upon affairs in their own time and relied on earlier authorities for information about previous ages. By and large, they lacked the intellectual and methodological means to employ original sources and to recover their meaning and significance. Instead, they depended upon the veracity of their predecessors. For this reason, history as a body of knowledge had little standing in medieval universities. No one could demonstrate with any reliability the truthfulness and believability of historical assertions. Subsequently, important changes took place between the fourteenth and nineteenth centuries. During those 500 years of turmoil and upheaval, history achieved the status of an academic discipline and obtained new capacities to verify its principal claims.


## RECOMMENDED READINGS


*Historians at Work,* Volume 1: *From Herodotus to Froissart,* edited by Peter Gay and Gerald J. Cavanaugh (New York: Harper and Row, 1972) provides a convenient anthology of the writings of the great historians in the ancient and medieval worlds. *The Ancient Historians* by Michael Grant (New York: Charles Scribners Sons, 1970) considers the Greeks and the Romans. Herbert Butterfield, *The Origins of History* (New York: Basic Books, 1981) describes the inception of historical thinking and Christian renditions. Contributions in the medieval period are considered in Joseph Dahmus, *Seven Medieval Historians* (Chicago: Nelson-Hall, 1982) and Indrikis Sterns, *The Greater Medieval Historians: An Interpretation and a Bibliography* (Washington, D.C.: University Press of America, 1981). John Barker, *The Superhistorians: Makers of Our Past* (New York: Charles Scribner's Sons, 1982) contains fine essays on Herodotus, Thucydides, and St. Augustine. A sophisticated and detailed study by Ernst Breisach, *Historiography: Ancient, Medieval, & Modern,* 2d ed. (Chicago: The University of Chicago Press, 1994) covers in much greater depth many of the issues under consideration here. The volume by John Gould, *Herodotus* (New York: St. Martin's Press, 1989), in a new series devoted to great historians, provides an introduction. Similarly, Ronald Mellor's *Tacitus* (New York: Routledge, 1993) describes essential things for modern readers. Finally, Donald R. Kelley, ed., *Versions of History from Antiquity to the Enlightenment* (New Haven: Yale University Press, 1991) contains excerpts from many of the most prominent historians.

## ENDNOTES

1. Quoted in Herbert Butterfield, *The Origins of History* (New York: Basic Books, 1981), 76–77.
2. Michael Grant, *The Ancient Historians* (New York: Charles Scribner's Sons, 1970), 10–11.
3. Herodotus, *The Histories*, translated by Robin Waterfield (New York: Oxford University Press, 1998); *The Landmark Thucydides: A Comprehensive Guide to the Peloponnesian War*, edited by Robert B. Strassler (New York: The Free Press, 1996).
4. Herodotus, *The Histories*, trans. Aubrey de Sélincourt (Baltimore: Penguin Books, 1954), 13.
5. Quoted in Grant, *Ancient Historians*, 78; Thucydides, *The Peloponnesian War*, trans. John H. Finley, Jr. (New York: The Modern Library, 1951), 14.
6. Quoted in Grant, *Ancient Historians*, 78.

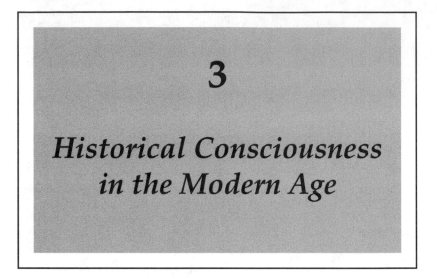

# 3

# Historical Consciousness in the Modern Age

The historical consciousness of the modern age developed gradually over the course of 500 years between the fourteenth and the nineteenth centuries. Fundamentally, the change entailed a transformation away from reliance on supernatural explanations and toward the development of secular approaches to the study of the past. Methodological constraints compelled such a shift. As historians came to realize, it was one thing to say with conviction that God acted in history and quite another to determine with any precision just where and when. History as a discipline acquired a more "scientific" outlook, at least insofar as methods of research, criticism, and analysis became more vigorous and acute and as practitioners tried to keep abreast of stunning advances in other areas of human knowledge.

In the modern age, history, much as other forms of academic inquiry, abandoned attempts to determine ultimate or final causes. Teleology fell into disrepute. The reasons are obvious and follow from the limitations of research methodology. No modern scholar working in a reputable field can claim legitimately to possess the means by which to verify any statements about the role of divine influences in the physical and historical worlds. As manifestations of faith, statements about God's purposes are not subject to proof by reason and evidence. Rather, they occupy a position in a different category of discourse. Consequently, historians as historians cannot with any veracity address such matters and must concentrate their efforts on devising methods by which to expand their understanding of the knowable world.

To such ends, historians have sought ways of enlarging in the present our comprehension of all kinds of artifacts from the past. In this sense, they attempted to recapture the spirit of the Greeks by approaching the study of history critically and putting more demands upon the evidence than upon the traditions of faith and authority. The transformation took place incrementally over a long period of time, beginning with the resurgence of interest in the ancient world during the Renaissance; reacting later to religious, scientific, and philosophical currents; and culminating with the establishment of university-based historical studies in the nineteenth century. During this formative period, Leopold von Ranke and other scholars changed the practice of history into a profession and laid down the main directions of development until the present day.

One of the first intimations of an impending break with medieval historiography occurred during the early stages of the Renaissance in the fourteenth century. The life labors of Francesco Petrarca, usually anglicized as Petrarch, aimed at the recovery of the traditions of ancient Rome. A native of the city of Florence in Italy, Petrarch devoted his attention to the preservation and transcription of classical writings. For him, the Roman experience incorporated the best attributes of humankind. "What else, then," he asked, "is all history, if not the praise of Rome?" Though concerned primarily with the collection of literary artifacts, he also wrote a history of Rome, *Lives of Illustrious Men,* and he contributed significantly to the establishment of a new, secular interpretation, but he did so without directly attacking Christian authority. His search for Rome set forth an alternative vision of human beings and their world in which real events had more than just symbolic importance. The actuality of human striving and attainment for him held great allure.

In the sixteenth century, another Florentine, Niccolò Machiavelli, focused attention on the human dimension in history through his writings on politics. Born in 1469 as the son of a lawyer, Machiavelli's education included readings in the Latin and Italian classics. Beginning in 1494, he embarked upon a political career when the combined effects of a French invasion and Girolamo Savonarola's religious uprising resulted in the ouster of Lorenzo the Magnificent, the ruler of Florence and a member of the house of Medici. Machiavelli subsequently served the Florentine republic in various capacities at home and in other states until the restoration of the Medicis in 1512. Forced into exile on a farm outside of the city, Machiavelli then spent his time trying to regain his lost influence and writing about the conduct of politics, the true description of which became his obsession. His most famous work, *The Prince*, set forth a body of precepts, showing that the actual methods of governance had little to do with medieval political theory. According to this handbook on the uses of political power, the wise prince had to know when to employ duplicitous or cynical means. Power and the proper utilization of it to achieve self-interested advantages constituted the great theme. History for Machiavelli turned into a kind of potpourri of examples by which to illustrate his maxims. His *History of Florence* detailed the intrigue and machination so characteristic of the politics of his own city and depicted actual behavior as a function of opportunism and aggrandizement.

The rediscovered wisdom of the Greeks and Romans inspired the Italians during the Renaissance and served them as models, especially the writing of Thucydides, Polybius, and Titus Livy. Following such leads, the ensuing narratives often dwelt upon political and military themes. Machiavelli's younger contemporary, Francesco Guicciardini, adhered to the classical themes in his *History of Italy*. A better historian than Machiavelli, Guicciardini carried out more research, notably in the papal archives; understood more subtly the diversity of human nature; and espoused a less provincial outlook. He examined the history of a country within a large geographic area, not a city; strove to obtain a broad, interpretive framework; and showed some of the connecting features in various aspects of Italian experience.

Though such historians addressed modern problems, various methodological shortcomings still impeded the development of a modern historical consciousness. Scholars had not yet developed appropriate methodological techniques for elucidating the meaning of historical artifacts within the context of their own times, places, and cultures. To be sure, antiquarians and humanists during the Renaissance collected and preserved Greek and Roman documents and by so doing inadvertently created repositories of immense value for future historians. But the more immediate interest centered on venerating the memory and emulating the style than in subjecting the ancients to analysis and interpretation. Philology, that is, the science of verifying and authenticating old manuscripts—now called *hermeneutics*—preoccupied them more than history. In this endeavor, the development of critical techniques made possible the identification of forgeries, alterations, and mistaken transcription.

A famous example involved a political fraud. According to a widely accepted myth in the late Middle Ages, Constantine the Great, the first Christian emperor of Rome, upon his conversion to the faith had bestowed religious and political authority over the Roman Empire in the West upon the bishop of Rome, in this case Pope Sylvester II. The popes in later years had invoked the legend as a basis for establishing their claims to power. In 1440, Lorenzo Valla proved the story false in a brilliant piece of detective work entitled *Discourse on the Forgery of the Alleged Donation of Constantine*. Using the methodologies of textual criticism, that is, philology, Valla demonstrated that the presumed substantiating document abounded with errors, inconsistencies, and anachronisms, showing that no one could have written the *Donation* in the fourth century. The faked document had to come from a later time.

The Protestant Reformation and the ensuing religious and political upheavals in the sixteenth and seventeenth centuries in Europe intensified the interest in history among the warring factions but made it the agent of partisan and polemical debates. Antagonists on all sides invoked the sanction of the past to give authority to their positions in the present. The issues centered on the role of the Church in interpreting the word of God to believers, the character of the Bible as a historical text, and the circumstances surrounding the development of Christianity as an institutional religion.

Protestants attacked their adversaries by insisting that papal control had corrupted the purity of belief and practice inherited from the early Church. In Germany, Martin Luther and his ally, Philip Melanchthon, used history to challenge Roman Catholic traditions. Somewhat later, a group of Lutheran scholars under Matthias Flacius Illyricus published a study of thirteen volumes entitled *Magdeburg Centuries* in an effort to document Lutheran assertions that the Roman hierarchy had distorted and perverted the teachings of Christ and the apostles. Similarly, Robert Barnes, an Englishman, wrote *Lives of Roman Pontiffs*, in which he ascribed an assortment of misdeeds and wrongdoings to high Church officials. Roman Catholics fought back, using history in defense of their beliefs and practices. In 1571, a papal commission chose Caesar Boronius to rebut the *Magdeburg Centuries*. According to his *Ecclesiastical Annals*, the various postapostolic changes obtained legitimacy as clarifications and interpretations of Christ's teachings and, in addition, as manifestations of the workings of the Holy Spirit.

Such controversies divided all of Christendom and resulted in the establishment of some of the first professorships in history at European universities. The Lutherans, for example, established one at Heidelberg and the Calvinists another at Leyden. Although such innovations contributed over the long term to the dissemination of professional history, a more immediate effect brought about the disintegration of uniform Christian interpretations of history and also a growing gap between sacred and secular forms of understanding. As a consequence of the Protestant Reformation, the consensus in support of St. Augustine's version of universal history ceased to exist, and no new, unifying approach emerged immediately as a replacement.

Meanwhile, the great scientific revolutions of the seventeenth century raised other unsettling questions about the problem of devising reliable and accurate accounts of the past. Following the discoveries of Newton, Kepler, and Galileo within the orders of nature, a scientific worldview took hold of European intellectuals, many of whom doubted the feasibility of obtaining verifiable knowledge in imprecise fields of investigation such as history. For philosophers schooled in the wonders of scientific discovery such as Descartes, Spinoza, and Leibnitz, mathematical formulations held the key to exactitude and certainty. As contemporary British historian B. A. Haddock observed, "Mathematics had removed the aura of mystery from nature, had freed enquiry from the obfuscation of medieval obscurantism, and it was thought that the same tool would be similarly successful in the study of man."

According to the champions of natural science, history as a discipline had failed in the development of verifiable methods. If historians could not express knowledge in approximate conformance with the mathematical ideal, then they had either indulged in a "harmless but irrelevant enjoyment of confused perceptions" or, much worse, embarked upon "a dangerous error in the path of truth." As Haddock noted, for the philosophers of natural science, "These mechanical methods were essentially timeless. They used a model of reason, eternally valid, based on their own mathematical procedures, which destroyed the validity of all other modes of experience."[1] They set before historians one of the great epistemological issues of the last four centuries, specifically, the degree to which the natural sciences can and should determine the forms of knowledge and understanding in the study of human affairs.

In spite of all the controversy over religion and philosophy, more pragmatically minded historians persisted in the production of significant and enduring works. In 1566, Jean Bodin, a French teacher of jurisprudence, published *Methods for the Easy Comprehension of History*, in which he called for an expansion of legal studies as a means of escaping provincialism. He wanted to create a new kind of universal history, comparing and contrasting the laws and customs of all nations. He employed complex categories, establishing distinctions among divine, natural, and human history and organizing the materials according to chronological and geographic criteria. He also insisted upon the preeminence of primary over secondary sources. A little over a century later in 1681, another Frenchman, Jean Mabillon, published two volumes entitled *On Diplomatics*. Pronounced a masterpiece in the twentieth century by no less an authority than the great French medievalist Marc Bloch, this study encouraged demanding scholarship while pursuing the methods and techniques of deciphering ancient charters and manuscripts and determining their authenticity—a science known at this time as "diplomatics." The detection of forged documents, of course, had practical significance both for historians and lawyers and could take on economic importance in disputes over land, property, and privilege. Through the use of comparative analysis, Mabillon proposed to identify error and inconsistency.

Such methodological tenacity was uncharacteristic in the seventeenth century. For example, in the same year, 1681, Bishop Jacques Bénigne Bossuet's *Discourse on Universal History* appeared as a means of teaching morality to the Dauphin, the male heir of King Louis XIV. Thematically reminiscent of St. Augustine, the *Discourse* affirmed tradition and authority by employing a providential view and depicting the Roman Catholic Church as the chosen agent of God's will. A kind of throwback, this work recalled a style of writing from a time before the Reformation, the scientific revolution, and the methodologies of diplomatics.

The era of the Enlightenment produced a torrent of historical writing with significant effects on historical thinking. In the eighteenth century, European philosophers proclaimed the advent of a new age of advancement for humankind. The attainment of enlightenment required an end of ignorance and superstition so that, henceforth, the facility of reason should govern the conduct of human behavior. As a kind of corollary, the movement also implied a rebellion against the authority of traditional religion. In a famous and important book, *The Idea of History*, British philosopher and historian Robin G. Collingwood characterized the Enlightenment as an attempt "to secularize every department of human life and thought." He saw it as "a revolt not only against the power of institutional religion but against religion itself." As Collingwood explained, Voltaire, a leading figure, regarded himself as the spearhead in a crusade against Christianity and other backward and barbarous influences. His slogan, "Ecrasez l'infâme," called upon his contemporaries to "crush the wicked thing."[2]

Meanwhile, competing tendencies appeared in the English-speaking world. An early attempt at critical history, William Camden's *Brittania*, published in 1586, focused on pre-Roman antiquity. It took on some of the attributes of later scholarship by depicting as false the heroic tales of King Arthur's time and also by espousing strong nationalism. According to one commentator, Camden "wanted to be both patriotic and scientific ... an enormous assignment, but he succeeded magnificently."[3] Another Englishman, transplanted to North America, engaged in an impressive exercise in writing contemporary history. William Bradford began *Of Plymouth Plantation* in 1630 and continued it for two decades. This spare, simple narrative provided the most complete story of the Plymouth colony on Cape Cod in Massachusetts during the early years. Bradford served as governor for a long time. His stark tale of anguish and adversity recorded the trials endured by the settlers and incorporated a message regarded by all Protestant Pilgrims as true. The hand of God directed human history in inscrutable ways. Another example of writing contemporary history emerged from the great religious and political struggles in England between the Puritans and the Cavaliers in the middle of the seventeenth century. This subject over the years has preoccupied many students of English history as a central and formative experience. An early account by Edward Hyde, the first Earl of Clarendon, entitled *History of the Rebellion and Civil Wars in England*, presented a passionate defense on behalf of the Church of England and the king against the assaults of tyranny, regicide, and irreligion.

Such issues produced deep divisions during the Enlightenment. The foremost historians—Voltaire, David Hume, and Edward Gibbon—disparaged the role of religion, depicting it as an impediment to human progress. For Voltaire, the priestly classes ranked among the great deceivers in all ages and in all places. Indeed, they functioned as the purveyors of bigotry, intolerance, and oppression. For Enlightenment historians, the liberation of people from religious superstition was a mark of human advancement toward rationality and emancipation.

Attempts to move beyond the customary categories also typified the writing of history during the Enlightenment. Secular writing ordinarily comprised political and military affairs and centered on the activities of Western Europeans. Voltaire most notably wanted an extension of the frontiers to encompass social, economic, and cultural dimensions and also the inclusion of non-Europeans. Indeed, he consciously composed some of the first social and cultural history and developed a kind of fixation on the Chinese.

In spite of such laudable impulses, much of the written history during the Enlightenment suffered from a fundamental flaw. It consisted of an incapacity to comprehend the behavior of historical actors on their own terms. The historians lacked a truly historical sense of development and context in the past. Locked into the precepts of their own time, they regarded their own values and aspirations as universal and absolute, the best toward which humankind could strive. Consequently, they tended to regard deviations in other times and other places either as aberration or folly.

Collingwood made the point pungently, arguing that "the historical outlook of the Enlightenment was not genuinely historical" at all. Rather, he described it as "polemical and antihistorical." Paradoxically, the past repelled historians, who interpreted it as a confining influence from which to escape. In Collingwood's words, historians regarded the past as "sheer error ... a thing devoid of all positive value whatever." Accordingly, the scholars had difficulty comprehending the past as the participants experienced it, and when gauged against the standards of the present, it failed to measure up. A related problem stemmed from a reluctance to carry out much archival research. Instead, the historians preferred to draw on existing works. As Collingwood remarked, "they were not sufficiently interested in history for its own sake to persevere in the task of reconstructing the history of obscure and remote periods."[4]

Voltaire, the very embodiment of the Enlightenment spirit, personified the problem. The author of an immense number of works in many different literary genres, he also figured prominently in the development of historical writing. First and foremost, he insisted that history should have a practical purpose. Pursued reflectively and philosophically (*en philosophe*), the study of the past should contribute to the cause of enlightenment by freeing readers from fallacy and misconception. Voltaire affirmed the point bluntly, claiming that "All ages resemble one another in respect of the criminal folly."[5] For the same reason, all merit historical study. Only by facing up to the shortcomings of the past could human beings achieve the necessary release. Voltaire intended further to write discriminating history, concentrating especially on "that which deserves the attention of all time, which paints the spirit and the customs of men, which may serve for instruction and to counsel the love of virtue, of the arts and of the fatherland."

Voltaire's principal historical works consisted of *Philosophy of History*, later incorporated as an introduction into *Essay on the Customs and the Spirit of Nations*, and his masterpiece, *The Age of Louis XIV*. In the first essay, employing in the title a term he coined, *philosophy of history*, Voltaire intended to illuminate the mind of his mistress, Madame du Châtelet. By depicting philosophically the human advance out of barbarism, he showed the malignant influence of priests among the Egyptians, Hebrews, and Christians. In effect, he turned medieval historiography on its head. But Voltaire put little stock in basing his claims on evidence. For him, reason and credibility, more than original documents, should provide the test of truth. For example, he questioned the story of Noah's ark by asking "how many persons were in the ark to feed all the animals for ten whole months, and during the following year in which no food would be produced?" The second volume depicted the late seventeenth century, the age of Louis XIV, as one of four ages of "great attainment" in the history of humanity and hence an object of special attention. The other three ages took place in Greece under Pericles, in Rome under Caesar and Augustus, and in Constantinople after the fall of the city to Mahomet II. His portrait of the many achievements in Europe during the reign of Louis XIV amounted to the invention of cultural history.

Though less a polemicist than Voltaire, David Hume, a Scotsman, shared the secular bent. Contemporary critics denounced his philosophical works as the products of skepticism and atheism. In contrast, his historical works won for him fame and fortune. His six-volume *History of England* was one of the best and most popular in the eighteenth century. Moving backward in time, as someone noted, much "as witches used to say their prayers," Hume wrote first about the Stuart kings, then the Tudors, and finally the invasion of Julius Caesar. Critical and iconoclastic in approach, Hume refused to put history in service to politics and wrecked romantic legends and patriotic myths. As a rigorous empiricist, he hesitated always to claim more than the observation of phenomena could warrant or to think that patterns of the past necessarily would recur in the future. Hume consequently found in history no particular sanction for any specific moral or legislative programs. Indeed, he mistrusted metaphysical claims and religious dogmatism as the breeders of fanaticism and instability. For him, the Puritan revolution against King Charles I was a case in point. Political equipoise required an ability to adapt institutions to the dictates of experience.

Perhaps the greatest of the Enlightenment histories, *The Decline and Fall of the Roman Empire* by Edward Gibbon covered a period of 1300 years from the first century until the Renaissance and ran to some million and a quarter words. Gibbon, an Englishman, spent twenty years of his life on the project but invested little effort in searching out new documents. Instead, he drew heavily on the works of seventeenth-century scholars and antiquarians. This colossal effort amounted to a synthesis of the existing research on the ancient and medieval worlds. It also transposed St. Augustine's thesis in *The City of God*. Rather than absolve the Christians of responsibility for bringing about the terrible events leading to Rome's fall, Gibbon held them primarily accountable. To simplify his argument exceedingly, Gibbon maintained that the obsessions of a hard-pressed people with life after death resulted in the neglect of imperial interests and the need to maintain proper defenses. Other-worldly concerns corroded the Roman will, undermined the Roman army, and brought about the collapse. In a kind of summary statement, Gibbon set forth the essentials of his view:

> The theologian may indulge the pleasing task of describing Religion as she descended from Heaven, arrayed in her native purity. A more melancholy duty is imposed on the historian. He must discover the inevitable mixture of error and corruption which she contracts in a long residence upon earth, among a weak and degenerate race of beings.[6]

This kind of condescension toward the past raised important methodological questions. Critics such as Robin G. Collingwood in the twentieth century attacked Enlightenment historians on the grounds that their insensitivity in effect violated the integrity of history. More specifically, they failed to empathize properly with the historical actors and to comprehend their behavior accurately on their own terms. Rather, Enlightenment scholars indulged in exposés, reviling the past to obliterate and overcome it. Consequently, Collingwood denounced their writing as an enterprise gone fundamentally wrong. They had failed to carry out the historian's primary task, that is, to elucidate the past, not merely to condemn it. For Collingwood, the magnitude of irresponsibility took on even greater proportions because a methodological means for achieving the goal already existed. Giambattista Vico, an obscure Italian theorist from Naples, had shown the way.

Vico published his brilliant and innovative book in 1725. Hailed in the twentieth century as the product of genius, truly an anticipation of modern social science, *The New Science* had much less impact on the eighteenth century. In discouragement, Vico himself lamented of his work, "it has gone forth into a desert." No one initially paid much attention, even though Vico had provided the methodological means for resolving the dilemma of the Enlightenment historians. To overcome the confines of one's own time and to treat the past with a proper degree of historicity, he demonstrated that scholars had an obligation to reconstruct the mental universe of people in previous times in order to account for their actions. Voltaire could have learned a great deal from Vico.

Vico presented *The New Science* as a critical response to the overblown and exaggerated claims in natural science. For example, René Descartes had disenfranchised history as a branch of knowledge because of the notorious unreliability of traditional accounts, in his view, a manifestation of fantasy and make-believe. Vico, in contrast, established an epistemology by which to set forth verifiable, true claims. While refraining from any denial of the validity of mathematics, he insisted upon the feasibility of other forms of knowing. To rebut Descartes' notion that the natural order constituted the most promising field for truthful inquiry, he insisted upon an intriguing idea, really, a kind of first principle. To understand anything fully, he argued, the observer must have made the thing under observation. Because God had created nature, only he could grasp the totality of it. In contrast, because human beings had made history, they possessed full capacity for arriving at a correct understanding, providing, of course, that they employed the right methods.

Vico conceived of history as a dynamic process of change, characterized by a movement through three stages. Though admittedly Eurocentric in design, the scheme at least rested on a recognition that different people in different places and different times actually saw and experienced the world differently. As a devout Christian, Vico adhered to the essentials of the Old Testament rendition until the aftermath of the Great Flood but then put his own stamp on the course of events. Noah's descendants, after some 200 years of chaos, embarked upon a journey through the age of gods, the age of heroes, and the age of men. Vico believed that human nature underwent changes during the progression and that identifiable links connected beliefs and institutions into a whole. During the first stage, an age of sensation, ferocity and cruelty typified human nature, and governments took on theocratic forms, thereby providing appropriate subordination to prevailing conceptions of deity, regarded as the cause of all things. During the second, an age of imagination, nobility and pride constituted human nature, and the government consisted of a warrior aristocracy. During this time, language, law, and culture developed, and mythic or poetic modes of consciousness became dominant. Finally, during the third, an age of reason, human nature emerged as reasonable and benign; governmental institutions evolved into egalitarian democracy, and a sense of reflective rationality governed human behavior. But Vico would not bask in pure optimism. He anticipated the possibility of returns to barbarism by imagining history as a spiral movement with cycles as part of the process.

For Vico, the proper means of studying history emanated from philosophy, that is, reasoning from axioms, definitions, and postulates, and from philology, the empirical study of the languages, history, and literature of people. Oddly, considering Vico's animus against Descartes, *The New Science* assumed the format of a geometry text, setting forth specific rules by which to obtain the truth. Among other things, he warned of prejudices conducive to error. Scholars should beware of exaggerating the grandeur of the past. They should recognize that all nations favor their own history at the expense of others. They should not assume that people in the past resembled them or that the ancients knew more about themselves than did current scholars. Vico proposed to employ the study of linguistics, mythology, and law as primary keys to unlock the meaning. Historians could never comprehend their predecessors unless they learned to see the people as the people viewed themselves.

For this purpose, Vico scrutinized the roots of words, folklore, tales, myths, legends, and legal systems for important clues. For Voltaire, a story about supernatural beings acting upon the human residents of the world signified ignorance and superstition. For Vico, in contrast, it provided a means of investigating the conception those people held of themselves and their position in the universe. By emphasizing context and self-perception, Vico produced an early version of some of the precepts of "historicism" in the nineteenth century. While Enlightenment thinkers liberated history from the constrictions of theology, Vico and his followers discovered methods by which actually to recover the past. In the nineteenth century, their disciples obtained a modern consciousness.

History in the nineteenth century became multifaceted, diffuse, and ever more rigorous methodologically. As a consequence, the study of history obtained respectability in the great European universities of the day and achieved the status of an academic discipline. Professionally trained historians ultimately dominated the field, but gifted amateurs and philosophers with an interest in history also contributed to three distinctive kinds of historical writing. One strand grew out of the struggles of the French Revolution and the Napoleonic Wars and emphasized a romantic and nationalistic approach. A second, most characteristic of Germany, perceived the flow of history as a subject for abstract, philosophical thinking. A third, a forerunner of today's university-based, professional history, aspired to find out what actually happened through careful investigations based upon archival research. The ensuing process of intellectual enrichment resulted in an era of significant attainment and overcame the most incapacitating shortcomings of Enlightenment history. Rather than manifest disdain for the past, the historians of the nineteenth century reveled in its diversity.

Romantic and nationalistic historiography predominated in France after the Bourbon restoration in 1815. Jules Michelet was a prime exemplar. As a self-conscious disciple of Vico, Michelet aspired to write the history of the French people. While using unconventional sources such as folklore, songs, poetry, and architecture, he proposed to develop portraits of everyday life. He identified with the common people. His six-volume *History of France* depicted and eulogized peasant life in the medieval period in vivid detail. It also exulted in the emergence of a sense of nationhood. Related themes appeared in Francois Guizot's *History of Civilization in France,* published in 1830. This expression of patriotic and romantic nationalism won fame for Guizot as a historian and also influence and power. He became the king's first minister under Louis Philippe. History and politics served together nicely in Guizot's case.

In England, Thomas Babington Macaulay also favored romance. As a prose stylist he had few equals. High-blown and self-consciously magisterial in the approved fashion of the nineteenth century, Macaulay's *History of England* obtained a wide audience and established history as a branch of great literature. It also articulated an uncompromising version of the Whig interpretation by treating the nation's story as synonymous with the emergence of liberty. As Macaulay wrote, "The history of England is emphatically the history of progress. It is the history of a constant movement of a great society." In sonorous and balanced cadences, the historian argued the case, applauding the triumph of the Glorious Revolution of 1688 over the Stuart despots, concluding that "the history of our country ... is eminently the history of physical, of moral, and of intellectual improvement."[7]

In the United States, the works of George Bancroft and Francis Parkman also set forth the themes of romantic nationalism. These great amateurs employed soaring prose for dramatic effects. Bancroft, like Guizot, combined careers in scholarship and public service. His writings told the story of national development, emphasizing the advance of liberty as recounted from the viewpoint of a Jeffersonian Democrat. In a series of books, Parkman's elegant prose reconstructed the conflict between France and Great Britain in North

America during colonial times. Parkman's *The Oregon Trail,* another sort of adventure, created a kind of nature poem. In contrast, Henry Adams's nine-volume *History of the United States during the Jefferson and Madison Administrations* aspired to the status of science. As the grandson of one president, John Quincy Adams, and the great-grandson of another, John Adams, the cosmopolitan and well-connected Henry Adams wanted to tell the nation's story and also to uncover the laws governing invariable relationships in human affairs. Although he later judged the latter part of his effort a failure, his work still ranks as a foremost scholarly attainment in the nineteenth century.

Abstract forms of philosophical history emanated primarily from Germany. They had deep roots in the eighteenth century. Johann Gottfried Herder and Immanuel Kant both wrote philosophical treatises on history. Herder's *Ideas toward a Philosophy of History of Man* described human life as closely related to nature and portrayed history as an evolutionary process. Each stage in the course of human development depended upon everything that had gone before. Otherwise, the latter stages could not occur at all. What existed in the present and what would come about in the future necessarily presumed whatever had been. This claim demolished the Enlightenment's habit of disparaging the past and compelled historians to appreciate the integrity of all eras. Herder particularly exulted in the varieties of human experience and extrapolated an important observation from them. According to Collingwood, he was "the first thinker to recognize in a systematic way that there are differences between different kinds of men, and that human nature is not uniform but diversified."[8] This view anticipated Collingwood's own conviction that people have no fixed nature. Instead, they have their history and become whatever historical experience makes of them. Collingwood held that true historical thinking can never exist without this rudimentary recognition.

Immanuel Kant, the elder of the two men, reacted negatively to these claims and wrote a critical response entitled "An Idea for a Universal History from a Cosmopolitan Point of View." As Herder's former teacher, Kant thought that the work of his student was wrongheaded and in need of correction. Though never concerned primarily with the study of history, Kant too favored a philosophical treatment of the subject. Harkening back toward

Enlightenment traditions, he rejected Herder's emphasis on human dissimilarities and proposed instead to regard the unfolding of history as "the realization of a hidden plan of nature" by which "all the capacities implanted by her in mankind can be fully developed." Less impressed with diversity than Herder, Kant dwelled upon uniformity. For him, history amounted to a process by which humankind became rational and hence fulfilled its fundamental nature. With this view in mind, the main task of the philosophical historians required that they comprehend the means and mechanisms for attaining the aim.

Georg Wilhelm Friedrich Hegel addressed the issue in an ornate body of writing intended to explain the whole of the experienced world. Defining nature and history as the manifestations of divine will in space and time, Hegel developed a complicated and inclusive philosophical system to make everything intelligible. Its very complexity defied summary and often put off practicing historians who doubted the usefulness and verifiability of Hegel's magnificent abstractions. His *Philosophy of History*, a series of lectures compiled and published after his death, pursued no less an ambition than to make the entirety of the human past comprehensible.

To begin a brief characterization, Hegel espoused profound religious commitments. In repudiation of Enlightenment thinking, he put God back into history through his interpretation of it as a logical and orderly process, resulting in the manifestation of divine will in time. As a consequence, the attributes of reason and freedom, identified as characteristics of divine spirit, would gradually encompass the world. To make the point in a different way, Hegel wanted to provide a kind of theodicy in which he would explain the ways of God toward his creation. For Hegel, the source of experienced reality first existed as an abstract ideal, later made actual in the world through the unfolding of divine will in time.

In Hegel's scheme, the mechanism of change bringing about the realization of divine will proceeded dialectically, and human minds could arrive at understanding by reasoning similarly. In his world of pure thought, all things gave rise to their opposites. Light had no meaning apart from dark. The same held true for high and low, sharp and dull, near and far. In like fashion, an idea, or a thesis, resulted in a counter proposition, or antithesis, and the ensuing debate produced a synthesis, which in turn became a thesis and set the whole thing in motion again. For Hegel, the dialectic not only characterized how thought progressed toward understanding but also how change actually took place in the material world. Confusingly, he added that the steps could take place out of logical sequence.

The march of history, nevertheless, produced changing levels of consciousness among human beings. In effect, their natures underwent alterations as a result of new forms of experience and awareness. To put it simplistically, they became more rational and more free. As Hegel explained, no people could attain the ends of history, that is, freedom and rationality, until they knew that they possessed the capacity to exercise such faculties. The consciousness dawned slowly. As Hegel observed, "the East knew and to the present days knows only that *One* is free [i.e., the oriental despot]; the Greek and Roman world, that *some* are free [i.e., the aristocratic elite]; the German World knows that *All* are free [under the legal structure of the monarchy]."[9]

Though Hegel believed that he had explained the forms and logic of historical development with proper regard for the facts, not many practicing historians ever adopted the Hegelian system or tried to work within its constraints. Nevertheless, the effects significantly influenced historical thinking in the nineteenth century. Most obviously, though Hegel shared with Kant an inclination to emphasize emergent rationality among humans, in many ways an equivalent of freedom, he also sided with Herder in his comprehension of human nature as malleable and bending, never fixed or final. It existed in a condition of becoming. Accordingly, different humans in different times and places had quite different natures. Hegel also favored Herder's holistic conception of the human past in which each phase maintained integrity as a prerequisite to whatever followed. For Hegel, the patronizing attitudes of the Enlightenment could only distort the past and prevent true understanding. As a means to obtain it, he insisted that historians must study bygone ages and epochs on their own terms.

These two points became central assertions of a school of historical thinking in nineteenth-century Germany. Termed "historicism" in English, an awkward translation of the German word *historismus*, this approach affirmed the need for particular methodological means to fathom the meaning of the past. Most fundamentally, it pointed to the diversity of human experience and claimed that as a consequence different peoples quite literally viewed the world differently. To comprehend their world, scholars had to enter into their mental universes empathetically and reconstruct their pictures of reality. Only by putting the past in context could scholars credibly explain the various forms of behavior. Knowledge of how the historical actors thought would facilitate an understanding of how they acted.

German historicists operated out of universities and spent their time in archives working with documents. By and large, they accepted Hegel's methodological advice but ignored or rejected his larger metaphysical system. It probably struck them as an a priori invention, neither proven nor provable. Rather than embark upon philosophically grandiose ventures, most of them embraced the more modest aim of writing history as it actually happened, or, to use the language of one of the foremost practitioners, *wie es eigentlich gewesen*. Leopold von Ranke wanted to describe historical events "as they really were." More than anyone, he transformed history into a modern academic discipline, university-based, archive-bound, and professional insofar as the leading proponents underwent extensive postgraduate training. The methods and techniques emanating from Germany spread elsewhere upon the continent, to Great Britain, and to the United States. They called for extensive research in primary sources to discover the truth, for detached and unbiased judgments, and for a determination by historians to see and to experience the world as it seemed to the historical actors.

Ranke's life work staggers the imagination. He lived ninety years and produced sixty volumes of published works. As the inventor of modern history, he chose the emergence of the European state system after the Reformation as his great theme. Working out of the University of Berlin for fifty years, his seminar method of instruction and his prolific scholarship made him world famous. George Bancroft of the United States on one occasion called him "the greatest living historian." Ranke stated his purpose in the preface to his *Histories of the Latin and Germanic Nations from 1494–1514*. "History has been assigned the office of judging the past, of instructing our times for the benefit of future years. This essay does not aspire to such high offices; it only wants to show how it had really been—*wie es eigentlich gewesen*."[10]

Ranke aspired to achieve balance and objectivity. Though on occasion his personal commitments to monarchy, Protestantism, and the Prussian nation state perhaps colored his judgments, his biases seldom destroyed his impartiality. Indeed, his works retain believability until the present day because of his comprehensive research and his scholarly disengagement. For example, his masterpiece, the *History of the Popes*, aroused criticism among contemporaries who thought it too bland and impartial. He also displayed great breadth. At age eighty-three, he set out to compose a universal history and managed to get through the fifteenth century before his death in 1885. For such prodigious effort and achievement, Ranke's legacy persisted into the twentieth century and profoundly shaped the professional writing of history.

Another strain of German thinking also retained an impact into the present day. As a young man, Karl Marx came under the influence of Hegel's idealism while pursuing advanced studies in philosophy at the University of Berlin. Though enamored of the dialectical construct as a logical device for describing change, Marx rejected the abstract and ethereal character of the Hegelian system. For Marx, reality resided in the physical world and not in idealistic forms as Hegel believed. According to Marx, Hegel's philosophy was backwards. Throughout his life, Marx aimed at rebutting Hegel's idealism with a new system of philosophical understanding based upon dialectical materialism. For him, it functioned as a way of comprehending the processes of historical change and establishing a basis for predictions into the future.

Marx focused attention on work, that is, the activity by which people obtained their livelihoods. He also examined the ensuing relationships with the means of production. Two ideas figured prominently in his thinking. For Marx, the reality of the class struggle characterized virtually the whole of human experience. In addition, a labor theory of value provided an essential key. Marx distinguished between the privileged elites who controlled the agencies of production and the unprivileged masses who labored in the fields and the factories. According to him, exploitation inevitably followed, because the former always appropriated a disproportionately large share of the wealth created by the investment of the workers' labor. For Marx, goods and commodities took on value because of the work required to make them. Farmers and workers produced valuable things and then had the proceeds taken away from them because of the workings of inequitable class relationships.

Much of Marx's writing sought to demonstrate the validity of his claims through investigations into the operation of European capitalism. His works also set forth predictions. Because of the very workings of history itself, Marx promised deliverance from want and oppression through the creation of a society without classes and exploitation. According to his explication, human experience consisted of a sequence of tumultuous upheavals in which vaulting technologies overturned established systems of production by rendering them obsolete and unworking all of the existing economic, social, and political relationships. Change, the enduring constant, proceeded dialectically and marked the measure of advancement, bringing human beings ever closer to a more perfect future, described by Marx as a condition in which all people would share more evenly in the rewards of their work. His visions of the future drew upon important legacies in the philosophy of history, going back to the Jews and the early Christians, but in this rendition, the course of secular history rather than transcendence would bring about salvation. Affirming a linear and progressive view of historical development, Marx put philosophy of history in service to the cause of revolution. As he once remarked, "the philosophers have only *interpreted* the world, in various ways; the point, however, is to *change* it."[11]

The Marxist injunction created immense divisions in the modern world over the proper understanding of politics, economics, and the role of history. While Marx and his followers issued the call to revolutionary action and sought legitimation in historical imperatives, more conventional and traditionalistic scholars held back from such leaps, refusing to employ their mode of investigation as justification for any vision of the future. Characteristically trained by the graduate schools in the importance of archival research and methodological and conceptual rigor, they hesitated to extrapolate their findings into the future, preferring to restrict their professional interests to presumably knowable subjects. To an extent out of caution and relief, historians left the predictive function to philosophers of history, who addressed it in imaginative and challenging ways.

## RECOMMENDED READINGS

*Historians at Work*, Volume 2: *From Valla to Gibbon*, and Volume 3: *Niebuhr to Maitland*, ed. Peter Gay and Victor G. Weller (New York: Harper and Row, 1972, 1975) make available samples of the writings of the great historians. Herbert Butterfield, *The Origins of History* (New York: Basic Books, 1981) traces the process of secularization. Additional commentary appears in Paul K. Conkin and Roland N. Stromberg, *The Heritage and Challenge of History* (New York: Dodd, Mead and Company, 1971). R. G. Collingwood, *The Idea of History* (New York: Oxford University Press, 1956) is indispensable. A revised edition of this work, edited and introduced by Jan Van Der Dussen (Oxford: Clarendon Press, 1993) includes previously unpublished lectures from the period 1926–1928. *History and Historians in the Nineteenth Century* by G.P. Gooch (Boston: Beacon Press, 1959, first published in l913); and *The Theory and Practice of History* by Leopold von Ranke, ed. Georg C. Iggers and Konrad von Moltke (New York: The Bobbs-Merrill Company, 1973) vividly depict developments during "the golden age" and make them accessible to English-language readers. Leonard Krieger, *Ranke, The Meaning of History* (University of Chicago Press, 1977) is a sophisticated intellectual biography using psychohistorical techniques. Interested readers also will benefit from *Leopold von Ranke and the Shaping of the Historical Discipline* (Syracuse University Press, 1990), ed. Georg C. Iggers and James M. Powell. John Clive, *Not By Fact Alone: Essays on the Writing and Reading of History* (Boston: Houghton Mifflin, 1989) is a delightful justification for reading the great historians of the nineteenth century. B. A. Haddock, *An Introduction to Historical Thought* (London: Edward Arnold, Publishers, 1980) surveys modern historical thinking and addresses the question of whether the models of natural science provide an apt basis for studying history. The book by Joyce Appleby, Lynn Hunt, and Margaret Jacob, *Telling the Truth about History* (New York: W. W. Norton, 1994) contains an illuminating discussion of science and history as ways of knowing.

Useful works on specific historians include Roy Porter, *Gibbon: Making History* (New York: St. Martin's Press, 1988); Patricia B. Cradock, *Edward Gibbon: Luminous Historian, 1772–1794* (Baltimore: Johns Hopkins Press, 1989); Nicolas Phillipson, *Hume* (New York: St. Martin's Press, 1989); Arthur Mitzman, *Michelet, Historian: Rebirth and Romanticism in Nineteenth-Century France* (New Haven: Yale University Press, 1990); John Clive, *Macaulay: The Shaping of the Historian* (New York: Alfred A. Knopf, 1973); and Owen Dudley Edwards, *Macaulay* (New York: St. Martin's Press, 1988). Herbert Butterfield, *The Whig Interpretation of History* (London: Penguin Books, 1931) remains illuminating. Isaiah Berlin, *Vico and Herder: Two Studies in the History of Ideas* (New York: The Viking Press, 1976) and Mark Lilla, *G.B. Vico: The Making of an Anti-Modern* (Cambridge, MA: Harvard University Press, 1993) establish appropriate intellectual contexts.

## ENDNOTES

1. B. A. Haddock, *An Introduction to Historical Thought* (London: Edward Arnold, 1980), 45.
2. R. G. Collingwood, *The Idea of History* (New York: Oxford University Press, 1956), 76.
3. Peter Gay and Victor G. Wexler, eds., *Historians at Work*, Volume 2: *Valla to Gibbon* (New York: Harper and Row, 1972), 84.
4. Collingwood, *Idea of History*, 77.
5. From "The Age of Louis XIV," in Gay and Wexler, eds., *Historians at Work*, 2:285.
6. In Gay and Wexler, eds., *Historians at Work*, 2:357. From Edward Gibbon, *The Decline and Fall of the Roman Empire*, ab. Moses Hadas (New York: Capricorn Books, 1962), 131.
7. Quoted in Gay and Wexler, eds., *Historians at Work*, Volume 3: *Niebuhr to Maitland* (New York: Harper and Row, 1975), 89; Thomas Babington Macaulay, *The History of England: From the Accession of James II*, 5 volumes (New York: A.L. Burt Company., n.d.), 1:2–3.
8. Collingwood, *Idea of History*, 90–91.
9. From the "Introduction" to Hegel's *The Philosophy of History*, in Monroe G. Beardsley, ed., *The European Philosophers from Descartes to Nietzche* (New York: The Modern Library, 1960), 553.
10. Quoted in Gay and Wexler, eds., *Historians at Work*, 3:16; Leopold von Ranke, *The Theory and Practice of History*, ed. Georg G. Iggers and Konrad von Moltke (New York: Bobbs-Merrill, 1973), 137.
11. Quoted in Bruce Mazlish, *The Riddle of History: The Great Speculators from Vico to Freud* (New York: Minerva Press, 1966), 227.

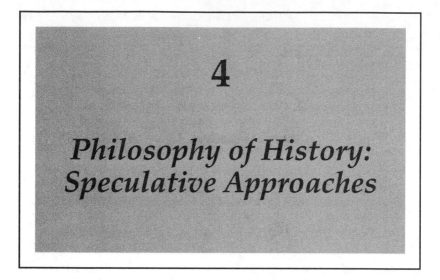

# 4

# *Philosophy of History: Speculative Approaches*

The term *philosophy of history* has acquired several connotations during the past three centuries. When Voltaire coined the term by insisting upon doing history *"en philosophe,"* he meant the construction of more meaningful narratives through the exercise of thoughtful reflection. Later the phrase took on different definitions. One encouraged speculation over the course and aims of history. This approach, the subject of this chapter, sought to obtain profound levels of truth by discerning patterns in the past and connecting them with expectations for the future. It required explanations that would aid in foretelling the goals and purposes of history on the supposition that students of history could know such things. A second version addressed in the next chapter, the analytical philosophy of history, has focused on problems in methodology, particularly in the areas of logic and epistemology. This approach has set forth rigorous standards and sometimes has scrutinized the degree to which historians and their actual practices have measured up. In combination, the emphasis on imaginative inquiry controlled always by fairness, reason, and evidence has contributed to intellectual richness in the discipline.

Human beings have ruminated about the directions of history since ancient times. Among other things, they have sought to mute their sense of vulnerability in facing the unknown by seeking to determine recurring tendencies in the past. Over the years, at least three basic schemata have characterized such endeavors, namely the cyclical, the providential, and the progressive. To be sure, variations on each have occurred, and imprecisions of usage have permitted the three to overlap and to intermingle. In spite of such confusions, each view retained a measure of distinctiveness. In the first, history moved in circles, repeating endlessly over and over again. In contrast, in the second and the third views, history comprised a linear process moving through time from a beginning to a middle to an end. The providential and the progressive versions each presumed some kind of advancement, or progress, through time but portrayed the impetus differently. In the providential view, divine guidance was the cause, and in the progressive view, natural or metaphysical forces were the impetus.

Manifestations of the cyclical idea arose among many ancient peoples and in some Eastern cultures. Egyptians, Sumerians, Babylonians, and Greeks by and large derived the premise from the orderly and predictable fluctuations of nature and attached little real significance to the passage of events. In a sense, they refused history. As noted by a historian of religions, Mircea Eliade, in his book *Cosmos and History: The Myth of the Eternal Return*, the inhabitants of traditional or "archaic" societies lived and operated in a kind of timeless present, a world very different from that apprehended by Jews and Christians. Though cyclical interpretations persisted even into the twentieth century, for example in a dazzling and perplexing work entitled *The Decline of the West* by Oswald Spengler, a German philosopher and historian, the more characteristic form of thinking in Western civilization has emphasized linear conceptions of the past.

A belief in providential design, affirmed so exhaustively by St. Augustine in the fifth century, appeared incessantly in the historical writing of the Middle Ages. This approach brought coherence to medieval chronicles by providing the means to fit contemporary records into the flow of universal history and also to express the faith in the reality of God's presence and purpose in the world. Sometimes unique formulations resulted in dramatic twists. Late in the twelfth century, Joachim de Flora divided history into three epochs, each corresponding with a figure in the Holy Trinity. The Age of the Father encompassed the pre-Christian era, the Age of the Son, the Christian era, and the Age of the Holy Spirit, an anticipation of the future. According to Joachim, each period would endure for forty generations, and the passage from one to the next would signify advancements toward conditions of greater wisdom, love, spirituality, and happiness.

The prophecy ironically took on revolutionary political implications after Joachim's death in 1202 by sparking interest among poor and humble people who aspired to a better life and promoted an upsurge of religious millenarianism, that is, an expectation of 1000 years of joy, serenity, prosperity, and justice.

A tripartite division of the past also appeared in Giambattista Vico's *The New Science*. A devout Roman Catholic, Vico tried to combine his belief in divine providence with a scholarly insistence upon the need for empirical investigations. By demonstrating the facts in particular cases, he would confirm the veracity of the larger whole. In his scheme of things, an amalgam of many elements, history advanced progressively through stages but also fluctuated in cycles, resulting in a kind of spiral effect. Vico perceived a three-tiered progression from "the age of the gods" to "the age of heroes" to "the age of men," and in each he detected holistic relationships among institutions, practices, and beliefs. Together they made up a uniformity. In his words, in the first stage, "the gentiles believed they lived under divine governments and everything was commanded them by auspices and oracles." In the second, "heroes...reigned everywhere in aristocratic commonwealths, on account of a superiority of nature which they held themselves to have," and in the third, "all men recognized themselves as equal in human nature and therefore there were established first the popular commonwealths and then the monarchies, both of which are forms of human government."[1]

Vico's extrapolation from these representations held that special forms of government, theocratic, aristocratic, republican, or monarchical, corresponded to each change, and moreover that particular kinds of language and jurisprudence necessarily resulted. For Vico, the various cultural parts interlocked at each stage, forming a coherent and uniform whole. In a summary statement, he further claimed that transformations took place in the makeup of human beings. In his view, "The nature of peoples is first crude, then severe, then benign, then delicate, finally dissolute." The cycles necessarily would run the whole course, each giving cultural expression to successive changes and then recurring on a higher plane, resulting in a progressive movement under God's supervision.

In the nineteenth century, Georg Wilhelm Friedrich Hegel endorsed some similar propositions. Indeed, he calculated the whole of his philosophical system to demonstrate the creative immanence of divine power in space and time. Nature and history for him served up the testimony. In what may have amounted to the most ambitious philosophical treatment of history ever attempted, Hegel set forth his views, defining a dynamic and rational process aimed at the attainment of reason and freedom. For Hegel, the course of history moved by comprehensible means toward the stated goal in a dialectical fashion. That is, the mechanisms of historical change required that ideas, or mind, generate reality by giving rise to opposites so that a constant tug-of-war went on between that which actually existed and that which might come about.

In somewhat different words, according to Hegel, history consisted of the means by which God achieved his purposes in the world and human beings arrived at new and higher levels of consciousness, both of their surroundings and of their own capabilities. The course of development moved generally from East to West from the Orient through the intervening regions to western Europe and took on institutional forms in the great religions and the apparatus of the state. Hegel espoused a provincial Eurocentric view, excluding Africa, the New World, and the Slavic domains from the course of history on the grounds that the inhabitants had not contributed much to the progress of humankind. In contrast, European regions, such as Greece, Rome, and Germany, had participated conspicuously. Hegel assigned special importance to World Heroes, his term for great men, who through the pursuit of their own interests actually served larger purposes. In quest of personal empire, Napoleon promoted European progress by sweeping away feudal remnants. Hegel attributed the unintended outcome to "the cunning of reason," his phrase for the capacity of divine power to manipulate historical actors in service to its own purposes.

The power of Hegel's intellect resulted in formidable attainments. The system defined a theodicy, that is, a justification of God's way toward humankind. Also, in Hegel's own view, it conformed with empirical proofs. Yet, more practical-minded historians regarded such constructs as the result not of hard facts but of unproven assumptions and a priori reasoning. The overwhelming inclusiveness of his philosophy of history, that is, his fierce determination to account for all things, would have placed unbearable strains on more orthodox historians seeking to work within such constraints. Very few scholars ever tried to compose their narratives within the confines of

Hegel's mental universe. Nevertheless, his contribution to historical thinking figured prominently, particularly in the emergent German historicist school, by depicting the flow of history as consisting of successive changes in the level of consciousness among human beings.

A shift toward secular characterizations of the past in progressive, linear terms achieved particular prominence during the Age of the Enlightenment in the eighteenth century. Typically these approaches set forth a preferred and favored vision of the future by which to bring about human redemption and then showed the necessary mechanisms driving history in that direction. The French contributed two notable exemplars. Voltaire explained history as a movement away from ignorance and superstition toward rationality and enlightenment. Somewhat similarly, in a work entitled *Sketch for a Historical Picture of the Progress of the Human Mind*, Marie Jean Antoine Condorcet early in the 1790s anticipated idyllic conditions at the end of ten developing historic stages, eventuating in "The abolition of inequality between nations, the progress of equality within each nation, and the true perfections of mankind."[2]

German thinkers also harbored progressive expectations. Immanuel Kant's *Idea for a Universal History from a Cosmopolitan Point of View* produced an important statement. Published in 1784, a decade before Condorcet's *Sketch*, this essay affirmed the expansion of freedom as the overriding purpose of history. According to Kant's argument, "the history of mankind viewed as a whole, can be regarded as the realization of a hidden plan of nature" by which to bring about the requisite political conditions both within states and among them so that "all the capacities implanted by her [nature] in mankind can be fully developed."[3] Although vague in explaining the manner of attainment, Kant envisioned the creation of an international league of nations as the prime institutional means by which to achieve order and rationality within the world under law.

For Kant, the study of history was not a central preoccupation. Nevertheless, according to the nine propositions set forth in this short piece, history moved inexorably toward the goal of liberty as a consequence of what Kant called "unsocial sociability." This energizing principle, really the driving force of progress, was in many ways the equivalent of Hegel's later idea, "the cunning of reason." Such formulations expressed a favorite notion of Enlightenment philosophers, who liked to think that the pursuit of private interests would somehow automatically translate into the advancement of the collective good. Kant intended the term to typify the devices employed by nature "to bring about the development of all the capacities implanted in men." Through the use of the term "unsocial sociability," he characterized a complicated process serving the general welfare in which social dynamics balanced countervailing tendencies toward integration and disintegration. As he explained in the fourth proposition, the "tendency" of human beings "to enter into society" appeared in conjunction "with an accompanying resistance which continually threatens to dissolve this society."[4] The ensuing creative tension resulted in progress.

To put this central claim another way, the conflicting and contradictory human needs to live together and to assert individual integrity paradoxically provided the momentum to move ahead. Typical of his time, Kant regarded stories about the past as consisting of lamentable tales of chaos, woe, disorder, and suffering. But in spite of the dismal record, he held forth better hopes for the future and intended his essay to hasten them along. In all likelihood, he wanted his writing to function as a kind of self-fulfilling prophecy as suggested by his choice of language in the eighth proposition. As the words reveal, he made no claim that history is "the realization of a hidden plan of nature," but rather said that it "can be regarded" as such. By implanting the thought, he hoped to encourage rational beings to act upon it as though it were true and thereby to attain the larger aim.

Another prophetic version appeared in the works of Karl Marx and his long-time collaborator, Friedrich Engels. Also linear and progressive in conception, their writings had an enduring and provocative effect. Unlike Kant, who only dabbled in the study of history, Marx and Engels devoted a large portion of their lives to the endeavor and from it fashioned a theory of change and revolution. Characteristically, they too devised a vision of a more perfect future, but unlike utopians, visionaries, and metaphysicians, whom they scorned, Marx and Engels believed that their analyses and predictions originated not in a priori imaginings but in a true comprehension of reality and a scientific understanding of historical development.

Their distinctive approach centered on crucial issues. First, Marx and Engels regarded the material world as the proper object of study, particularly the technologies of production and the economic, political, and social relationships generated by them. For Marx and Engels, the ownership of the means of production, that is, the tools, the lands, and the factories, established the main determinant of everything else. Second, Marx and Engels focused attention on a conception of class, defined in economic terms as ownership of property or lack thereof. As affirmed in *The Communist Manifesto*, their thesis held that all history has been "the history of class struggles" between the exploited and the exploiting, between the dominated and the dominating classes at various stages of social development. [5] Last, they articulated an explanation of historical advancement and also of the mechanisms producing it.

Also Eurocentric in orientation, the Marx and Engels formulation resembled Hegel's in some respects. It depicted a historical movement from the East to the West and also an expansion of the levels of human consciousness. Marx, of course, reversed Hegel's view by vesting reality in the material rather than in the ideal world, but he accepted the dialectic as defining the logic for the means of change. The ensuing term, *dialectical materialism*, put a label on Marx's assumptions about both. His subsequent division of the past into four great epochs had less to do with actual time periods than with his understanding of the various sets of human relationships in different systems of economic production. In some cases, they might even coexist.

The overarching pattern discerned by Marx entailed the persistence of exploitation throughout all of history. It always pitted the "haves," the wealthy and the powerful, against the "have-nots," the poor and the vulnerable. It also featured systematic and institutional methods amounting to thievery by which the former relieved the latter of the just rewards of their labor. For Marx, the amount of work invested in anything established the true value, but under the prevailing conditions the members of the labor force never received their just recompense. Instead, the ruling class appropriated the riches to its own use.

Marx posited the existence in the beginning of time of an age of primitive communism, marked by Garden-of-Eden–like qualities of simplicity, equality, and communal sharing; but then the Marxian equivalent of original sin, the advent of private property, shattered the idyll. Subsequently in Asia, the age of oriental despotism also featured an absence of private property and concentrations of population in small, dispersed, isolated communities under absolute rulers. Marx regarded such forms as dead, unchanging artifacts, receptive only to developments imposed from the outside. His real interest centered on Greece, Rome, and Western Europe, from which he derived a model marking the progression from the ancient to the medieval to the modern world. In ancient times, the class struggle took place in city-states and aligned slave owners against slaves. During the Middle Ages, the competition took the form of feudalism and divided lords and serfs over the ownership of land. In Marx's own day, the capitalist system set the owners of the means of production, the bourgeoisie, against the wage laborers, the proletarians, in the culminating conflict of interest and aspiration. According to Marx's calculations, the ensuing great revolution would overcome injustice and oppression through the abolition of private property and eventually would usher humankind into the new age of freedom and equality under the communist system in which all people would benefit from a fair distribution of the rewards of their labors.

Marx's depictions of the past and his expectations for the future provoked storms of criticism. Many scholarly works have claimed that his understanding of the ancient and medieval worlds suffered from fundamental flaws and that his other appraisals drastically overrated the revolutionary potential of modern times. Yet, his vision has retained the power to captivate in some circles, and many authorities agree that Marx knew more about the workings of nineteenth-century capitalism than almost anyone. Moreover, his insistence upon the need to study technology as an impetus toward transformation and change conveys an essential insight.

To simplify the general line of argument substantially, Marx asserted that the dominant, ruling class in any given epoch, that is, the males in charge of the technologies of production, also obtained control of political, legal, and social structures in order to safeguard their positions and interests. According to him, government officials in effect made up the board of directors of the economic ruling class. In similar fashion, legal arrangements, the social structure, and most other forms of organized human intercourse reflected the distribution of economic power. At the same time, the dynamism of historical imperatives threatened to unwork the status quo. Again and again in human history, the development of new technologies destabilized existing relationships and produced upheavals, rendering the old structures obsolete. For example, when the owners of factories obtained economic power, the former ruling elites, the feudal lords, struggled to retain their control of the political, legal, and social systems, but they could not withstand. The very logic of history had doomed them. Once triumphant, the bourgeoisie erected suitable forms by which to preserve and maintain their ascendancy.

For Marx, all historical eras gave rise to exploitation and class oppression but nevertheless possessed integrity as necessary steps in the march toward communism. The attainment of perfection could never ensue without the necessary, foregoing prerequisites. For Marx, the model achieved truth from empirical proof and also from the irrefutable force of its logic. For Marx's critics, in contrast, the prophetic faith in revolution perhaps held less interest than the holistic analysis of human affairs and the explanation of the processes of historical change. Some even agreed that no need exists to embrace all of Marx in order to profit from his explication of the workings of economic capitalism.

Old-fashioned, speculative philosophy of history lost some of its appeal in the twentieth century, in part because of the traditional, grandiose aims. In an age of highly specialized inquiry in which, according to a well-known quip, we learn more and more about less and less, hard-nosed observers put little faith in any attempt to account for the whole of the human past. Indeed, they regarded such endeavors as silly or contemptible, idle enterprises based on pure imagination and incapable of proof or demonstration. Although many scholars turned their attention to other things, the older versions never died out. Indeed, they lived on, oftentimes in somewhat modified form. Marxian legacies amalgamated with the ideas of Vladimir I. Lenin and retained an intellectual and revolutionary appeal in various quarters around the world. Oswald Spengler and Arnold Toynbee composed universal and philosophical histories. Sigmund Freud produced a body of speculative writing with significance for historians, and religious thinkers such as Reinhold Niebuhr took an approach to history that evoked memories of St. Augustine.

In the twentieth century, Marxist ideology became the official version of the past in communist countries and purported to present hopes for a better future in others. In hybrid form with Leninism, it held special importance as a theory of international relations according to which modern capitalist nation-states act in the world arena primarily for economic reasons. Seeking cheap resources, investment outlets for surplus capital, and new markets to relieve overproduction at home, the capitalist powers by this critique would always engage in a chronic struggle for profit and advantage, sometimes colliding in armed conflict, until the victory of revolution would sweep away all need for such practices. During the 1960s a group of historians in the United States called "the New Left" challenged the orthodox accounts of American foreign relations by arguing that models inspired by Marxist-Leninist thinking allowed for some insight into the international behavior of the United States. In their view, the United States was not necessarily an exception to European standards after all. A vociferous debate over the origins of the Cold War particularly occasioned a polemical duel when radicals claimed that the expansive nature of U.S. capitalism contributed significantly to the onset. In more recent times, a debate over "dependency theory" as an explanation for the plight of poor countries in the Third World has yielded similar intensity. Initially a product of Latin America and a variant of Marxist-Leninist thinking, dependency theory attributed the pervasiveness of poverty and underdevelopment in many places to the requirements of a global capitalist system designed to drain away wealth from the provincial and colonial regions to the advanced metropolis. By this analysis, the ascendancy of a world capitalist economic system will always result in oppression and exploitation. Although the end of the Cold War has now altered the context of the discussion, questions of development and modernization as understood in historical perspective no doubt will retain significance into the future.

In a similarly deterministic but more pessimistic fashion, Oswald Spengler, a morose, brilliant, and eccentric German prophet from the era of the First World War, harbored no apocalyptic visions of salvation or progress. The title in English of his erudite two-volume work set the tone. *The Decline of the West* resurrected the cyclical view of history and argued the case that no means of exit permitted any escape from the dictates of destiny. Spengler identified culture as the proper unit of historical study. Though somewhat vague in his definition, he claimed the existence of eight distinctive cultures over the course of human history. He called them the Indian, Babylonian, Chinese, Egyptian, Mexican, Arabic, Classical, and Western. The distinguishing feature, according to Spengler, consisted of "a single, singularly constituted soul." In a confusing, mystical flight, Spengler affirmed, "A Culture is born in the moment when a great soul awakens out of the protospirituality of ever-childish humanity, and detaches itself, a form from the formless, a bounded and mortal thing from the boundless and enduring." In elaboration, he asserted, "It blooms on the soil of an exactly-definable landscape, to which plant-wise it remains bound. It dies when this soul has actualized the full sum of its possibilities in the shape of peoples, languages, dogmas, arts, states, sciences, and reverts into proto-soul."[6]

Spengler further compounded the difficulties by regarding culture as the analogue of an organism in the biological world, fated to pass through the phases of birth, youth, maturity, old age, and death. Sometimes, as an alternative, he used the images of spring, summer, fall, and winter. Each one had a life span of about 1000 years and also displayed structural equivalences in the development of the life cycle. Spengler proposed to study them through the use of comparative morphology. This term, derived from the study of anatomy, referred to the form and structure of living organisms. Through the use of such techniques, Spengler intended to move beyond shallow comparisons to profounder insights. By this method, he concluded, Napoleon and Alexander the Great represented morphological "contemporaries," in that both stood in the same phase of a declining culture.

Spengler distinguished among the various cultures on the basis of diverse conceptions of time and space. An expression of cultural determinism, Spengler's provocative and revealing approach stated that each distinctive culture dictated a different standard for perceiving and measuring time and space. Each culture thereby obtained uniqueness but at the same time cut off and isolated the human beings in any one of them from all the others. Spengler put little stock in the possibility of meaningful cross-cultural transfers. Any such attempt could only result in inexplicability. To work out the ramifications of his case, he concentrated his attention on three cultures, namely the Classical, the Arabic, and the Western, each with "souls" characterized as Apollinian, Magian, and Faustian.

Spengler's discourses typically described the prevailing conceptions of time and space within a culture and then marshaled a parade of illustrations from the worlds of mathematics, drama, architecture, politics, economics, and so forth to substantiate his claims. According to him, the Classical or Apollinian soul most cherished the qualities of closed space and timelessness in the present and attained those ideals preeminently in nude statuary and Euclidean geometry. The Arabic or Magian soul in contrast organized impressions around a sense of cavernous space and time spans with clear beginnings and ends. As examples, Spengler cited the early Christian caves, Muslim mosques, and the Judeo-Christian linear designs of history. Finally, the Western or Faustian soul conceived of pure and limitless space and time stretching out into infinity, represented by differential calculus, museums, clocks, and presumably space shots to Mars.

Whatever the observable variations, according to Spengler, all cultures must share a common fate. Destiny requires that they run their life course and die. On this point, Spengler curiously used the language of astrology. In the German title of his work, *Der Untergang Des Abendlandes*, the first word has astrological significance, suggesting the decline or setting of the sun. As noted by one commentator, Bruce Mazlish, Spengler's sense of inevitability required foreordained outcomes because they are "in our stars." Mazlish referred to Spengler as "an astrological historian" for whom "Real history is heavy with fate but free of laws." As Mazlish remarks, "we can *divine* the future but not reckon or calculate it."[7]

Such bizarre oddities abounded in Spengler's writing. Though Spengler possessed a doctoral degree, he never obtained an academic appointment and mainly carried out his endeavors as an independent scholar. Perhaps his status as an outsider, thus removed from the mainstream of intellectual life in the universities, accounted for some of his quirks. His contemptuous disdain for other scholars and his pretentious boasts of an originality never previously attained rubbed many readers the wrong way. But Spengler struck a mood in the confusing years after the First World War and signaled a dramatic shift away from the sentimental optimism of the Victorian age.

Arnold Toynbee, an Englishman and a contemporary of Spengler, also suffered the effects of historical trauma during the Great War between 1914 and 1918. Seeking to render historical study more systematic and compelling, he inaugurated an ambitious project in 1920. Upon the completion in 1954, Toynbee's majestic twelve-volume work surveyed the whole experience of humankind and set forth a series of general propositions by which to convey the meaning. *A Study of History* ran parallel to Spengler's book in some respects but diverged in others. Most notably, Toynbee developed a particular interest in exploring the origins of civilizations and claimed to arrive at conclusions while adhering to the requirements of English empiricism—that is, while allowing the evidence to direct his findings and speak for itself. Though Toynbee professed aversion to the a priori techniques of his German counterpart, his critics later flailed him for falling far short of the aim, charging that he unwarrantably designated the Greek and Roman worlds as the models of all civilization and that on occasion he twisted the evidence to make it fit into his preconceived theories.

The Toynbee approach sought to obtain high levels of generality by depicting "societies" or "civilizations" as the proper units of historical study. Toynbee preferred them to nations or periods, because they partook of a more intelligible, larger whole. Though vague definitions caused problems for him and discrepancies in usage disorganized his count, Toynbee detected nineteen or twenty-one civilizations during the preceding 6000 years. Five still lived, our own Western civilization and also the Orthodox Christian, the Islamic, the Hindu, and the Far Eastern. The nonliving included the Hellenic, Syriac, Indic, Minoan, Sumeric, Hittite, Babylonic, Andean, Mexic, Yucatec, Mayan, and Egyptian. Finally, two sets of "fossilized" relics maintained remnants in the present, comprising Jewish and Buddhist traditions. Toynbee reasoned that a majority of civilizations emerged from some kind of a predecessor and that others developed directly from primitive life. The problem of explaining the genesis especially intrigued him. He rejected racial considerations and circumstances of nature as inadequate in accounting for the change and found the key in his conception of "challenge and response." As observed by D. C. Somervell, who abridged Toynbee's mighty work into two more accessible volumes:

> A survey of the great myths in which the wisdom of the human race is enshrined suggests the possibility that man achieves civilization not as a result of superior biological endowment or geographical environment, but as a response to a challenge in a situation of special difficulty which rouses him to make a hitherto unprecedented effort.[8]

In Toynbee's analysis, civilizations took shape when demanding challenges brought forth creative human responses. Toynbee emphasized the importance of "the golden mean." Too severe a challenge could overwhelm all manner of reactions and render them futile. Conversely, too bland a challenge would obviate any need to generate a response. For example, according to Toynbee, the ease of life in the South Pacific failed to elicit a response leading to high levels of civilization. In contrast, the efforts of Viking emigrants from Norway, which succeeded in Iceland, subsequently collapsed in Greenland upon encountering even tougher conditions.

Growth within a civilization, according to Toynbee, occurred when successive challenges met with creative responses. The responsibility for devising them resided with "creative minorities," that is, small groups of talented people who inspired others to follow them with the force of their example. The ensuing process, dubbed *mimesis* by Toynbee, impelled the masses of people to imitate their natural leaders. When mimesis ceased to exist or the minority elite lost its creativity, then "a time of troubles" descended upon the society, suggesting the possibility of a breakdown.

Toynbee rejected strictly deterministic solutions to the problem. No inevitabilities required the disintegration of societies. Nevertheless, his scrutiny of the process showed that the transformation of creative minorities into merely dominant minorities and the emergence of an internal proletariat, which felt "in" but not "of" the society, signaled dangerous, impending schisms. Though spiritual resources always have done a great deal to dictate the outcomes, Toynbee thought that social decomposition came about not in a uniform fashion but by an alteration of "routs" and "rallies," his terms for defeats and recoveries. As Toynbee explained, the establishment of a universal state, such as the Roman Empire, represented a rally after a rout in a time of troubles, and the dissolution of a universal state indicated the final rout. Somewhat oddly, Toynbee believed that he had detected a rhythm in the process, consisting of three and a half beats: "rout-rally-rout-rally-rout-rally-rout." Claiming to have confirmed the pattern through his investigations into several extinct civilizations, he wondered whether it applied to his own. In the abridgement, Somervell suggested that it might by remarking, "As differentiation is the mark of growth, so standardization is the mark of disintegration."[9]

In Toynbee's last four volumes, religious themes became a dominant motif. Though convinced that his own civilization had advanced far into a time of troubles, thereby heralding the possibility of a decline and fall, he retained some hope that spiritual rebirth might halt the descent through the affirmation of a more creative alternative. In this philosophy of history, no deterministic laws compelled any particular outcome. Everything depended upon the human actors, and religious conviction would function as the prime arbiter. In the concluding volumes, Toynbee emerged more as a religious thinker than as a historian.

A quite different influence upon the philosophy of history took shape early in the twentieth century in the writings of Sigmund Freud. As the founder of psychoanalysis, Freud was not primarily a historian. Nevertheless, Freud developed an approach to the study of human behavior with immense implications for history. Rather than concentrate on large collectivities, such as "cultures" or "civilization," he worked as a therapist, counseling individual patients and then extending his findings and insights into larger human domains. Though critics have attributed fundamental errors to him, claiming that he misinterpreted the sexually repressed mores of turn-of-the-century Vienna as universal characteristics, his champions, in contrast, have argued that he uncovered hidden fundamentals at the core of human nature.

Freud discovered the motive force of individual behavior in the psyche, that is, the internal mental life of all persons. In order to comprehend the function of this governing mechanism, he divided the mind into two parts, the conscious and the unconscious. The former, situated in the brain, produced deliberate and calculated thoughts, resulting in intentional acts to achieve designated goals and purposes. The latter, the more remote and inaccessible, by its very nature, lacked any awareness of itself but contained a resolution to the entire mystery.

To make possible an understanding of an otherwise impenetrable phenomenon within the unconscious, Freud posited the existence of three functions. First, the *id*, the oldest of the psychical provinces, consisted of inherited instincts and contained a cauldron of consuming drives, lusts, desires, and cravings, all of which sought expression in forms unknown to the person possessed of them. Second, the *ego* mediated between the demands of the id and the realities of the external world. To an extent, it defined the available range of possible forms of satisfaction, usually within the context of seeking after pleasure and avoiding pain. The third, the *superego*, performed something like the role of a conscience, deriving authority from mothers, fathers, and other such sources. More specifically, it perpetuated the experiences of childhood by prolonging into adulthood conceptions of right and wrong derived from "the personalities of the actual parents" and also from "the family, racial, and national traditions handed on through them, as well as the demands of the immediate social milieu which they represent." As Freud further explained, "the id and the super-ego have one thing in common: they both represent the influence of the past—the id the influence of heredity, the super-ego the influence, essentially, of what is taken over from other people—whereas the ego is principally determined by the individual's own experience that is by accidental and contemporary events."[10]

The interaction and competition among these three components accounted for the unconscious mental life of all persons. Freud ranked the experiences of childhood as central. The relationships with parents and siblings and other such events, often long forgotten but still stored away in the recesses of the psyche, determined adult behavior in ways usually unrecognized by the human actor. Mild disturbances, obsessions, compulsions, and the like, called *neuroses*, required treatment through psychoanalysis, a technique administered by a trained practitioner to make the patient fully conscious of hitherto unconscious psychical activity. Through the ensuing confrontation between the known and the unknown, a resolution of the remembered events with the unconscious traces should result in a cure. For drastically disarranged mental states called *psychoses*, Freud had more doubts about the possibilities of effecting much improvement.

Many of Freud's favorite phrases and ideas have become part of the jargon of the twentieth century. These include repression, projection, wish fulfillment, the analysis of dreams, the Freudian slip, and the Oedipus complex. Indeed, his emphasis on human sexuality as the source of the libidinal energy driving human beings has passed into current folklore. In contrast, his speculative writings on historical subjects have attracted less general attention but at the same time have spurred a consuming interest in some quarters among specialists who hope to achieve deeper levels of understanding through the use of psychoanalytical history.

Freud's books, *Totem and Taboo* (1912), *Civilization and Its Discontents* (1930), and *Moses and Monotheism* (1939) set forth suggestive models. Each concerned an analysis of psychical events derived from clinical observations and relationships with the external world. As Freud explained, he wanted to study "the interactions between human nature, cultural development and the precipitates of primeval experiences." Religion figured prominently in these considerations and reflected "the dynamic conflicts between the ego, the id, and the super-ego, which psychoanalysis studies in the individual."

In *Totem and Taboo*, Freud combined some of the theoretical reflections of Charles Darwin with his own clinical observations. Freud borrowed a hypothesis holding that human beings originally lived in small hordes, each under the absolute rule of an older male who took all the females for himself and brutalized and killed the younger men, including his own sons. Such patriarchal oppression came to an end when the sons collectively rose in rebellion, destroyed the father-tyrant, and consumed his flesh. Consequently, the young males constituted a totemistic brother clan in which taboos forbade sexual contact with the women in favor of exogamy. Moreover, collective ambivalence over the killing of the father resulted in the adoption of a totem. Usually an animal, it stood for their ancestor, now transformed into a spirit protector. The males would allow no one to hurt it, except in a ritual once a year when the whole clan feasted upon the creature. According to Freud, "it was the solemn repetition of the father-murder in which social order, moral laws, and religion had their beginnings." For Freud, the actuality of any such event held little consequence. Whether real or fantasy, the psychic impulse to kill the father would have had the same outcomes.

Similar characteristics marked *Civilization and Its Discontents* and *Moses and Monotheism*. In the former, Freud engaged in the speculative philosophy of history by musing about the direction of historical movement, particularly the transition from the religious to the scientific stage in human existence. Though ethnically Jewish, Freud never embraced the religious traditions of his heritage and, indeed, subjected them to merciless criticism. All religions he classified as mass delusions, unhappy and misguided efforts to substitute a wish fulfillment for an unbearable reality. In this work, he called upon human beings to give up childish responses and stoically to face the truth. In *Moses and Monotheism*, he elaborated upon a related theme, claiming provocatively that Moses, actually an Egyptian, "chose" the Jews, led them out of bondage, and shaped them into a holy nation. But the Jews, reacting against the Mosaic laws, murdered their leader and thereby reenacted the tribal horde experience with similar consequences, except in this instance a monotheistic conception of deity replaced the totem.

Such inferences outraged more orthodox thinkers and have retained a capacity to disturb until the present day. Indeed, an animated controversy has drawn the line with Freud's champions on the one side, insisting that psychoanalytical history can arrive at more profound appraisals of human behavior, and the critics on the other, rejecting his approach as a theory, neither proven nor provable. Perhaps most tellingly, the skeptics have depicted the techniques of Freud and his disciples primarily as therapies for which the only test of truth is practical. Does the patient get any better? If so, the practitioner has chosen the proper means of treatment and has arrived at a kind of truth. Unhappily, the historians employing psychoanalytical methods in their studies of dead people have no such means of verification and often have to indulge in speculative ruminations. Whether their inferential leaps illuminate the subject or obscure it remains an issue under fierce debate.

In conclusion, a final example illustrates the persistence of fundamental issues in discussions of speculative philosophy of history. In the United States during the 1940s, Reinhold Niebuhr attained formidable rank as a theologian, philosopher, and political commentator. A "neo-orthodox" Protestant in his religious commitments, Niebuhr set forth new versions of the Christian view but operated steadfastly within the larger traditions of St. Augustine.

For Niebuhr, neither the classical nor the modern secular renditions of philosophy of history held much merit. The Greek cyclical idea deprived history of real meaning by denying the significance of particular events. By submerging them in recurring patterns, according to Niebuhr, the Greeks denied to themselves the capacity to act creatively within the context of particular instances and sought to escape into an abstract world of pure thought, thereby transcending history altogether. In contrary fashion, the Western, linear, progressive construction of history put undue faith in the creative powers of human beings and found in history itself the means of attaining desirable goals, such as controlling nature, advancing human well-being, and democratizing society. In other words, the very course of historical development in itself would result in human betterment through the enhancement of freedom and good.

Because the modern version found meaning in the details of historical existence, Niebuhr held it in higher regard than the classical, but he also believed that it suffered from a serious error by assuming a necessary connection between the growth of human freedom and good. For Niebuhr, no such relationship had ever existed. Indeed, to the contrary, the growth of human freedom and power simply "enlarges the scope of human problems" by giving greater opportunity for the expression of "egotistic desires and impulses." As examples, he noted that:

> Modern industrial society dissolved ancient forms of political authoritarianism; but the tyrannies which grew on its soil proved more brutal and vexatious than the old ones. The inequalities rooted in landed property were levelled. But the more dynamic inequalities of a technical society became more perilous to the community than the more static forms of uneven power. The achievement of individual liberty was one of the genuine advances of bourgeois society. But this society also created atomic individuals, who, freed of the disciplines of the older organic communities, were lost in the mass; and became the prey of demagogues and charlatans who transmuted their individual anxieties and resentments into collective political power of demonic fury.[11]

Such views so typical of Niebuhr showed his compelling taste for irony and paradox. Things seldom have turned out as people intended. Nevertheless, according to him, Christian conceptions of history guarded against naively optimistic expectations by espousing a more realistic and valid understanding of human nature. Christians knew the reality of original sin. This condition meant that, in the course of time, human beings could neither achieve their purposes consistently nor utilize their freedom and power to attain good. Nevertheless, Niebuhr insisted that the sovereignty of God presided over the whole of the human experience. As Niebuhr put it, "All historical destinies are under the dominion of a single divine sovereignty," which provides a "general frame of meaning for historical events." Moreover, Niebuhr denied that either reason or evidence could confirm such a claim. Only an affirmation of the Christian faith could result in the certainty that "history is potentially and ultimately one story."

Niebuhr strove to work out the implications of his position in two important works during the 1940s, *The Nature and Destiny of Man* and *Faith and History*. These stood as Christian rejections of modern secularists, such as Marx and Freud, and returned the ancient debate to stark essentials. Niebuhr insisted on meaning in history but found the ultimate source of meaning outside of history. Similarly, by rejecting the feasibility of rational or empirical demonstration, he removed the arbiter of debate from history to theology. Faith would have to decide. By such means, he closed the circle with St. Augustine.

## RECOMMENDED READINGS

A useful compilation is available in Ronald H. Nash, ed., *Ideas of History*, Volume 1: *Speculative Approaches to History* (New York: E.P. Dutton, 1969). Bruce Mazlish, *The Riddle of History: The Great Speculators from Vico to Freud* (New York: Minerva Press, 1966) provides good introductory essays. Additional commentary exists in Frank E. Manuel, *Shapes of Philosophical History* (Palo Alto: Stanford University Press, 1965); Karl Löwith, *Meaning in History: The Theological Implications of Philosophy of History* (Chicago, IL: University of Chicago Press, 1949); and Peter Munz, *The Shapes of Time: A New Look at the Philosophy of History* (Middletown, CT: Wesleyan University Press, 1977). In *The Poverty of Historicism* (New York: Harper and Row, 1957), Karl R. Popper argues against the possibility of predicting the future. Introductions to Marx include David McClellan, *Karl Marx: His Life and Thought* (New York: Harper and Row, 1973); M. M. Bober, *Karl Marx's Interpretation of History* (2d ed. rev.; New York: W. W. Norton, 1965); Melvin Miller Rader, *Marx's Interpretation of History* (New York: Oxford University Press, 1979), and Gerald Allan Cohen, *Karl Marx's Theory of History: A Defense* (Princeton, NJ: Princeton University Press, 1978). *Telling the Truth about History* (New York: W. W. Norton, 1994) by Joyce Appleby, Lynn Hunt, and Margaret Jacob, contains a series of fine essays concerned with the emergence of modern historical consciousness.

Useful specialized works appear in Isaiah Berlin, *Vico and Herder: Two Studies in the History of Ideas* (New York: The Viking Press, 1976); Mark Lilla, *G. B. Vico: The Making of an Anti-Modern* (Cambridge, MA: Harvard University Press, 1993); William A. Galston, *Kant and the Problem of History* (Chicago, IL: University of Chicago Press, 1975); and Burleigh Taylor Wilkins, *Hegel's Philosophy of History* (Ithaca, NY: Cornell University Press, 1974). *The New Psychohistory* (New York: Psychohistory Press, 1975), ed. Lloyd de Mause, sets forth a ringing defense. More critical works by Jacques Barzun, *Clio and the Doctors: Psycho-History, Quanto-History & History* (Chicago, IL: University of Chicago Press, 1974) and David E. Stannard, *Shrinking History: On Freud and the Failure of Psychohistory* (New York: Oxford University Press, 1980) raise important questions. Some compelling answers in Freud's defense appear in Peter Gay, *Freud for Historians* (New York: Oxford University Press, 1985). Freud's own book, *An Outline of Psycho-Analysis*, trans. James Strachey (rev. ed.; New York: W. W. Norton, 1969) provides a resume of his thought. *The Irony of American History* (New York: Charles Scribner's Sons, 1952), by Reinhold Niebuhr, sets forth some of the main themes.

Biographical works of special significance in addressing these topics include Richard Wightman Fox, *Reinhold Niebuhr: A Biography* (New York: Pantheon Books, 1985); Peter Gay, *Freud: A Life for Our Time* (New York: W. W. Norton, 1988); and William H. McNeil, *Arnold J. Toynbee: A Life* (New York: Oxford University Press, 1989).

## ENDNOTES

1. Quoted in Bruce Mazlish, *The Riddle of History: The Great Speculators from Vico to Freud* (New York: Minerva Press, 1966), 38. See also *The New Science of Giambattista Vico*, revised translation of the third edition (1744), trans. Thomas Goddard Bergin and Max Harold Fisch (Ithaca,NY: Cornell University Press, 1968), 335–351.
2. Mazlish, *The Riddle of History*, 90.
3. In Ronald H. Nash, ed., *Ideas of History*, Volume 1: *Speculative Approaches to History* (New York: E. P. Dutton, 1969), 61.
4. Nash, ed., *Ideas of History*, 2:54.
5. In Karl Marx, *The Communist Manifesto* (Chicago: Henry Regnery Company, 1954), 13–15.
6. Quoted in Mazlish, *Riddle*, 336; Oswald Spengler, *The Decline of the West*, ab. Helmut Werner (New York: The Modern Library, 1962),73–74.
7. Mazlish, *Riddle*, 320.
8. Arnold J. Toynbee, *A Study of History*, ab. D.C. Somervell (New York: Oxford University Press, 1957), 2:357–358
9. Arnold J. Toybee, *A Study of History*, 2:589.
10. Sigmund Freud, *An Outline of Psychoanalysis*, trans. James Strachey (New York: W. W. Norton, 1949), 16–17.
11. Reinhold Neibuhr, *Faith and History* (New York: Charles Scribner's Sons, 1949.) Copyright renewed 1977 Ursula M. Neibuhr. Reprinted with permission of Charles Scribner's Sons.

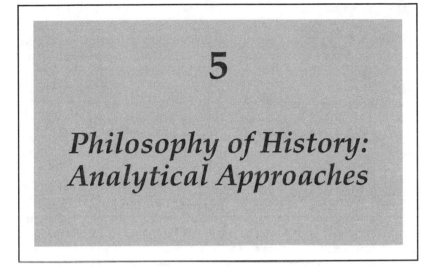

# 5

# Philosophy of History: Analytical Approaches

The development of analytical or critical philosophy of history in the twentieth century has affected a quite different set of concerns. This branch of intellectual inquiry has addressed issues in methodology and epistemology, centering particularly on the crucial question: On what grounds can historians reasonably demonstrate that they know what they claim? In other words, the verifiability of historical knowledge comes under review. In pursuit of this discussion, one kind of criterion measures the logic, rigor, and techniques of history against the prevailing forms in the natural sciences. Other items under consideration include the formal requirements of an explanation, the meaning of causation, and the role of objectivity. Such issues have posed persistent problems and have elicited an ongoing debate nowhere near resolution. Nevertheless, they have vital significance in comprehending the theoretical dimensions of the discipline.

The main lines of division go back at least into the seventeenth and eighteenth centuries, when Francis Bacon, René Descartes, and other scientists tried to establish more reliable means for studying the natural world. They and their successors favored mathematical formulations for testing and expressing their findings; they also liked high levels of generality by which to affirm statements of invariable relationship. This latter phrase refers to recurring uniformities and regularities among phenomena. In rudimentary terms, such statements took the following form. Whenever some combination of prior conditions existed in a particular instance, then a certain and predictable kind of outcome necessarily would follow. To utilize an example from nature, whenever fire heated water to the proper temperature and in the right circumstances, then surely steam would come about as a consequence.

Although the actual statements of invariable relationship became more intricate as the problems under observation grew more complex, the formal logical structure underlying them remained more or less constant, and for many natural scientists, the greater extent to which they could express them in mathematical terms, the better. Ordinarily the formal logic connected the anterior or preceding conditions to the observable outcome by means of affirming a general, empirical law. It said simply that, after repeated verifications through experimentation, whenever those kinds of conditions came into being, the same outcome or consequence would take place. Put crudely in categories more congenial to historians, the invocation of a general law meant that, given the same causes, very similar effects almost surely would occur.

Giambattista Vico in the eighteenth century repudiated such methods as inappropriate to historical studies, but the ascendancy of scientific models overwhelmed his objections nevertheless and resulted in a flatly dogmatic assertion. It held that all forms of knowledge must conform with the methods and techniques of natural science or else forfeit any rightful claim to the status of knowledge. Those presumably inferior kinds of inquiry, those less demanding in logical form or less mathematical in orientation, would have two choices: Either measure up against the dictates of "the hard sciences" or suffer disparagement as pseudoscience. For serious students of human affairs, the dilemma conversely left open two courses of action. First, they could conform with the demand, emulate the natural sciences, and seek to present their findings as general statements of invariable relationship. Such endeavors later would lead to the developments of the social sciences. Second, they could insist on the propriety and integrity of the traditional methods and techniques within their own fields of study, disclaiming any need to adhere to the models of the natural sciences. This latter affirmation sometimes depicted history as *sui generis*, that is, a class of learning unto itself.

A modern version of the debate appears in a book by Robert William Fogel and G. R. Elton entitled *Which Road to the Past? Two*

*Views of History* (1983). It draws a tentative distinction between "scientific" and "traditional" history with Fogel, a distinguished economic historian, championing the former, and Elton, a noted authority on Tudor England, the latter. As friendly intellectual rivals, neither scholar wishes to disenfranchise the other as the possessor of a valid form of knowledge. Nevertheless, they favor distinctive versions. Fogel argues for the utility of social scientific models and mathematical formulations in order to obtain higher-level general truths about the past. Elton, in contrast, wants historians to do what the good ones have always done—that is, examine the existing evidence without preconceptions and then establish rational judgments about what it means.

Historically the controversy achieved special prominence in the middle of the nineteenth century with the advent of positivism. Primarily the work of Frenchman Auguste Comte but subsequently embraced and elaborated upon by two Englishmen, Henry Thomas Buckle and John Stuart Mill, this body of thought sought to transform the study of human affairs into a more systematic sort of inquiry by endorsing the techniques of natural science. Rather than focus on unique or individual kinds of events, positivists proposed to concentrate attention on uniformities and similarities in the course of human affairs and then to locate the invariable relationships linking the same kinds of experiences. Rather than study the French Revolution, they would investigate the phenomenon of revolution. In so doing, positivists presumed the existence of general laws governing the outcomes of activity in the human world, just as in the natural world, and they put their trust in their own intellectual capabilities to find them.

The works of Auguste Comte gave rise to sociology and established the essentials in ten mighty volumes, *Cours de philosophie positive* (six volumes, 1830–1842) and *Système de politique positive* (four volumes, 1851–1854). To an extent, Comte's philosophy grew from his personal experiences, some of them a bit bizarre. Indeed, he obtained central insights leading to the Law of the Three Stages, a fundamental tenet, while suffering one of his periodic bouts with madness. The victim of an unhappy home life as a child, Comte fled to study mathematics at the École Polytechnique in Paris, abandoned Roman Catholicism, and for a time came under the influence of the French utopian socialist, Henri de Saint-Simon. Though degrees of instability and eccentricity always marked Comte's personal life and sometimes found expression in unique forms of religiosity, for example, his commitment to a religion of humanity, he possessed the intellectual means to set forth an entire philosophical system called *positivism*.

Comte began with the familiar division of the past into three parts, claiming as a basic premise that the human mind had developed historically through three stages. Straightforwardly Eurocentric, he intended to focus his attention on the "vanguard of the human race," by which he meant the inhabitants of Italy, France, England, Germany, and Spain. He also preferred to proceed at a high level of abstraction, espousing his wish to employ history, except for reasons of stark practicality, "without the names of men, or even of nations." One commentator, historian Bruce Mazlish, explained that this "dehumanization of history" came about because Comte really took primary interest in the sciences and their development. Ranked in ascending order of difficulty according to Comte, these included mathematics, really nothing more than a logical tool; astronomy; physics; chemistry; physiology, now called biology; and at the pinnacle, sociology.[1]

A basic proposition affirmed the Law of the Three Stages by which Comte showed that the evolution of the human mind took place in three steps. He derived many of his convictions from the histories of the foregoing bodies of knowledge. In each, the affirmations about reality progressed from the theological through the metaphysical to the positive stages. In the first, human beings saw the world as controlled by wills independent of their own but subject to propitiation or manipulation by prayer or magic. During the second, abstract forces, such as the requirements of nature or the will of the people, governed all things, and in the third, the positive and final stage, an understanding of the invariable relationships among phenomena would provide for the explanations.

Much in the fashion of various predecessors, Comte also presumed holistic relationships, affirming that each mental stage corresponded with other kinds of intellectual and institutional developments. The theological phase, for example, coexisted with military life and primitive slavery, the metaphysical with lawyers and attempts at creating governments based on law, and the positive with industrialism. But Comte's complicated efforts at refinement and elaboration also allowed them to overlap, so that mathematics, the simplest among the forms of knowledge, could achieve positive status in the otherwise theological age. But sociology, the most complex of all as the science of human beings, could attain the position only when all other forms of learning had also progressed to such a rank.

In the positive stage, no need would exist to indulge in idle speculation over first or final causes. Instead, positivist principles would concentrate full attention on knowable subjects and the elucidation of lawlike regularities that affirmed invariable relationships among phenomena. These in turn would not rely upon theological or metaphysical presumptions but upon empirical observations from the real world. Once advanced up the ladder of learning from mathematics to astronomy to physics to chemistry to biology, the positivist philosophy would result in the creation of a new human science, sociology, the articulation of which would culminate in new kinds of understanding of the laws governing human behavior and consequently in new certainties over how best to calculate the probable outcomes of deliberate human acts.

The declaration of a positivist philosophy by Comte, Buckle, and Mill produced a strenuously adverse reaction. Usually called "idealist" within the context of this debate, this school of thought emanated from the writings of Wilhelm Dilthey, a German; Benedetto Croce, an Italian; and Robin G. Collingwood, an Englishman. Collectively they argued that the analogy derived from the natural sciences could not hold up under the test and that the intricacies of writing history required quite different conceptual schemes. Late in the nineteenth century, Dilthey drew a fundamental distinction between the natural sciences (*Naturwissenschaften*) on the one hand and the human sciences (*Geisteswissenschaften*) on the other. The practice of each called forth distinctive methodologies. For one thing, according to Dilthey, the natural scientist sought regularities and uniformities in nature upon which to base generalizations, while the historian dealt with unique, specific, and unrepeatable events outside of nature. For him, the difference between the general and the particular meant everything.

Later on in the twentieth century, Croce, one of Italy's most important intellectuals, and Collingwood, an Oxford philosopher, historian, and archeologist, elaborated on the idealist conception of history. Croce emphasized the all-important consideration that historians existed in the present. For the past to take on vitality and meaning, historians had to make it come alive with relevance by re-thinking it in their own minds. For this reason, Croce drew the con-clusion that "All history is contemporary history." Collingwood, often provocative and crotchety but seldom eccentric, dedicated his life to setting forth the fullest and most enduring statement of the idealist position. His great book, *The Idea of History*, published posthumous-ly after his death in 1943 at age fifty-two, still ranks among the most significant books on the philosophy of history ever published in the English language.

To begin, Collingwood described history as "the science of human nature," the aim of which aspired to "self-knowledge." For him, the deceptive simplicity of that statement meant that the prop-er object of historical study centered on the human mind, or more properly the activities of the human mind, and further that the ap-propriate means of investigation required "the methods of history." To employ a different phraseology, historians learned about the mind by comprehending what the mind had done. Collingwood then dis-cussed the disparity between the methods of the natural sciences and the human sciences and explained why the former had no analogous relationships with the latter. "The historian, investigating any event in the past, makes a distinction between what may be called the out-side and the inside of an event." With these words, he established the very crux of his message.

By the "outside of an event," Collingwood meant "everything belonging to it which can be described in terms of bodies and their movements: the passage of Caesar, accompanied by certain men, across a river called the Rubicon at one date, or the spilling of his blood on the floor of the senate-house at another." By "the inside of an event," he referred to that "which can only be described in terms of thought: Caesar's defiance of Republican law, or the clash of con-stitutional policy between himself and his assassins." To highlight the difference, Collingwood conceded that "The historian is never concerned with either of these to the exclusion of the other." As he ex-plained, the work of the historian "may begin by discovering the out-side of an event, but it can never end there; he must always remember that the event was an action, and that his main task is to think him-self into this action, to discern the thought of his agent."

Collingwood then set forth another main thesis. "In the case of nature, this distinction between the outside and the inside of an event does not arise." He stated, "The events of nature are merely events, not the acts of agents whose thought the scientist endeavors to trace." In other words, what takes place in nature manifests no inner life. "To the scientist, nature is always, and merely, a 'phenomenon'...a spectacle presented to his intelligent observation." For the historian, in contrast, "the events of history are never mere phenomena, never mere spectacles for contemplation, but things which the historian looks, not at, but through, to discern the thought within them."

Collingwood then summarized his point by putting it still another way. In seeking to penetrate "to the inside of events and detecting the thought which they express, the historian is doing something which the scientist need not and cannot do." Nevertheless, the methodological prescription for attaining the goal produced great problems. How shall the historian make certain of the thoughts acted out by human beings? According to Collingwood, "There is only one way in which it can be done: by re-thinking them in his own mind." Or, as he affirmed in another place, "The history of thought, and therefore all history, is the re-enactment of past thought in the historian's own mind." This creative and critical experience "reveals to the historian the powers of his own mind" and hence of all minds, resulting in a fuller appreciation of human nature as revealed by the mind while working on actual experience.[2]

For positivist critics, the idealist position partook of fantasy, mysticism, and self-deception. It called for explanations based on the operation of an unobservable entity called mind and required empathetic leaps into the heads of historical actors, all of which depended upon faith, not science. Under the criteria of the idealist alternative, the historian would know only when knowledge became knowable, and no other test would set forth a standard. For Comte's disciples, this premise lacked methodological integrity, defied verifiability through the use of evidence or observation, and belonged properly in the metaphysical stage of human development.

For Collingwood and his followers, in contrast, the appropriate rejoinders put down positivist charges on several grounds. First, idealists insisted that they possessed methodological integrity, claiming that their approach, if carried out prudently and rigorously, indeed, allowed for verifiable insights into the workings of mind. Through the correct use of documentary evidence, that is, letters, diaries, and the like, the historian could make legitimate inferences. Second, they

regarded the role of active, critical thought about the past as significant. Only by such means could they bring life into history. Collingwood denounced dullish recitations of mere facts based on earlier
authorities as "scissors-and-paste history." Finally, Collingwood had
no use for the positivist emphasis upon the need for generalization.
As he remarked in an important passage, "If, by historical thinking,
we already understand how and why Napoleon established his ascendancy in Revolutionary France, nothing is added to our understanding of that process by the statement (however true) that similar
things have happened elsewhere." To reenforce the point, he added,
"It is only when the particular fact cannot be understood by itself that
such statements are of value."[3]

The controversy between positivists and idealists has become a
dominant issue in philosophy of history and has permeated virtually all discussions of historical methodology. Divergent conceptions of
explanation, causation, and objectivity bear directly on the matter and
demonstrate additional aspects of the contemporary debate. These
show further some of the complicated ramifications of historical thinking, thereby lending even more credence to an observation by philosopher W. H. Walsh, who noted that in truth "history is an altogether
stranger and far more difficult discipline" than it is often taken to be.[4]

Another philosopher, Carl G. Hempel, established the main categories under discussion in 1942 with the publication of his seminal
essay, "The Function of General Laws in History." In this presentation
of the positivist case, Hempel argued that the explanatory forms of
natural science indeed held true in the field of history. While defining a general law as "a statement of universal conditional form which
is capable of being confirmed or disconfirmed by suitable empirical
findings," he described the main function as "to connect events in
patterns which are usually referred to as explanation and prediction."
A quotation from Hempel will indicate the line of reasoning:

> The explanation of the occurrence of an event of some specific kind E
> at a certain place and time consists, as it is usually expressed, in indi-
> cating the causes or determining factors of E. Now the assertion that
> a set of events—say, of the kinds Cl, C2,..., Cn—have caused the event
> to be explained, amounts to the statement that, according to certain
> general laws, a set of events of the kinds mentioned is regularly ac-
> companied by an event of kind E. Thus, the scientific explanation of the
> event in question consists of

1. a set of statements asserting the occurrence of events Cl,... Cn at certain times and places,
2. a set of universal hypotheses, such that
   a. the statements of both groups are reasonably well confirmed by empirical evidence,
   b. from the two groups of statements the sentence asserting the occurrence of event E can be logically deduced.

The ensuing analysis, though complicated and difficult to follow upon first encounter, arrived at an emphatic conclusion. It held that "The preceding considerations apply to explanation in history as well as in any other branch of empirical science." As Hempel affirmed, "Historical explanation, too, aims at showing that the event in question was not 'a matter of chance,' but was to be expected in view of certain antecedent or simultaneous conditions." Although in some instances "the universal hypotheses underlying a historical explanation are rather explicitly stated," Hempel conceded that, more characteristically, most "fail to include an explicit statement of the general regularities they presuppose" because "they are tacitly taken for granted" or they lack "sufficient precision." As he noted, affirmations about the movement of Dust Bowl farmers to California in the 1930s have assumed a "universal hypothesis" to the effect that populations in times of hardship "will tend to migrate to regions which offer better living conditions." By omitting the authority of a general law, historians have employed what Hempel called "an explanation sketch."[5] Though incomplete in detail, it had to adhere, nevertheless, to the logical requirements of the explanation form.

The controversy has consumed analytically minded philosophers of history ever since. Dubbed "the covering-law model" by critic William Dray, the Hempel position called upon historians to explain specific events by subsuming them under a general proposition. But dissenters found little point in doing so and rejected such advice on several grounds. First, they noted that the actual practices of historians seldom conformed with Hempel's prescription. Indeed, they argued, to follow it would render the entire exercise banal because of the absence of meaningful and agreed-upon general laws in the field of history. Either such generalizations do not exist or the lack of precision and specificity would deprive them of exactitude. Would anyone acquire a new and deeper understanding of the French Revolution by explaining that the French have always acted that way?

Another criticism recalled Collingwood's critique. William Dray and others pointed out that the task of historians required them to make actions comprehensible within the context of the historical actors' own motives and aspirations. Once having accounted for the reasons for an act, the historian has nothing left to do.

In 1962, Hempel published another essay, seeking to meet the various attacks and to fend them off through tactical accommodations. This time he dealt more directly with the actual writings of historians and allowed them some greater degree of flexibility. According to his array of definitions, the "probabilistic-statistical form" of explanation maintained "to the effect that if certain specified conditions are realized, then an occurrence of such and such a kind will come about with such and such a statistical probability." The "elliptic or partial" explanation sketch presupposed the existence of general laws but failed to invoke them explicitly, and the "genetic explanation" accounted for changing conditions in history by linking them systematically to earlier ones. But in each instance, Hempel still insisted upon holding the historians to the requisites of what he now called "deductive-nomological explanation" forms, asserting in good positivist fashion that "the nature of understanding... is basically the same in all areas of scientific inquiry." Indeed, he claimed to his own satisfaction to have demonstrated "the methodological unity of all empirical sciences."

The problem of understanding the nature of causation in history also intrudes upon the matter. The term *cause* has always produced perplexity. Historians usually have employed it in a kind of commonsense fashion so that ordinary readers have access to their discussions, but nevertheless their ambiguities and imprecisions of usage have distressed logicians and philosophers. At least one authority, an Englishman, Michael Oakeshott, has recommended dropping the use of the term altogether.

To illustrate the manifold grounds for confusion, Aristotle once distinguished among four types of cause. They comprised the material, efficient, formal, and final. Among them, according to Ronald Nash, three have particular relevance to the study of history. An "efficient" cause consists of the prior events and conditions required for the occurrence of the main event, often by producing the needed energy. For example, according to Nash, an observer might describe the cause of Abraham Lincoln's death as the bullet fired into his head by the assassin John Wilkes Booth. A "formal" cause in history accounts for an event through the location of "dispositional properties" needed to bring it about. As Nash notes, a window might break because glass is brittle, or in Lincoln's case, death occurred because of the hatred of Booth and other Southern sympathizers for him. Last, a "final" cause accounts for an event by attributing it to the will or purpose of an agent. In this instance, Lincoln died because Boothe wanted to eliminate him in order to bring about more generous treatment of the defeated Confederacy.

Advocates of the positivist and idealist schools also divide sharply over this question. The former, as adherents to the covering-law model, must regard cause in the "efficient" sense as the most appropriate to history. Obviously, their preferred explanation form compels them to think of cause as a set of prior events and conditions. Moreover, as a kind of corollary, they usually conceive of cause as energy, a sort of mechanistic notion derived from physics. Just as the impact of the cue ball impels the eight ball into the side pocket in pool, so the combined effects of population pressures and land scarcities compelled people to move to the great American West. Idealists, in contrast, usually have understood the term in the sense of "final" cause. For them, it necessarily meant the will or intention of the historical actors. Purposeful action became the key. Once having ascertained Brutus's thoughts while stabbing Caesar, the historian could aspire to nothing else.

Still another difficulty has compounded the problem. While discussing causation, analytical philosophers often have established distinctions between "necessary" and "sufficient" conditions in accounting for the course of human events. Necessary conditions entail probabilities. A statement of them refers to the minimum requirements necessary to allow an event to take place. The focus centers on likelihood rather than certainty. Sufficient conditions in contrast involve inevitabilities. A statement of them would amount to a guarantee that a certain outcome will result. Because historians usually debate the causes of big and complicated events, such as the fall of the Roman Empire or the onset of the First World War, they seldom can handle all the variables under consideration. As a result of the limitations of intellect, historians most often traffic only in necessary conditions. Their narratives, rightly understood, almost always ponder probabilities, almost never inevitabilities.

The last issue under discussion in this chapter addresses the nature of objectivity. Often described as the most important and the most difficult methodological problem facing historians, objectivity as traditionally conceived requires that scholars withdraw personal preferences to the extent possible and seek to describe the subject under consideration as accurately as possible. But the degree to which historians have attained the goal and indeed can ever hope to do so has resulted in profound disagreements. A study by Peter Novick, *That Noble Dream: The "Objectivity Question" and the American Historical Profession* (1988) explores the matter. Though the contours of the debate do not follow strictly the positivist–idealist cleavage, the two positions still suggest some of the magnitudes of difference.

The positivist argument once again would hold the historians to the standards of natural science by insisting that any other option will result in a diminution of rigor and believability. To demand anything less would disqualify history from the ranks of empirically based, scientific disciplines and relegate it to the status of pseudoscience, perhaps on a par with alchemy and phrenology. Yet, such criteria pose special impediments because they often presuppose a resort to laboratory techniques by which natural scientists seek to exclude variable factors and to exert maximum controls. Such procedures presume a large measure of repeatability. That is, anyone carrying out the experiment in the same way and under the same conditions ought to arrive at the same findings and conclusions.

For historians, this conception of objectivity presents two immediate obstacles. First, historians do not work in laboratories and can neither exclude confusing variables nor control other conditions. For obvious reasons, their objects of study compel quite different approaches. Moreover, the idea of repeatability has less bearing. Indeed, a reverse kind of consideration has come into play. Among "hard scientists," history and other "soft" sciences in human studies are sometimes viewed as suspect, mainly because the scholars have difficulty arriving at solid agreements and confirming one another's findings. Though certainly overstated, according to this stereotype, if ten historians scrutinized the same bodies of evidence, they probably would arrive at ten different versions of meaning and significance. In this case, what critics might regard as disorder and disarray, the historians in all likelihood would view as signs of intellectual vitality. The body of literature on almost any historical subject takes the form of an ongoing debate.

Whether this aversion to consensus has reduced history to the status of pseudoscience has precipitated even more dissension. Some historians, inclined toward a relativist persuasion, have argued that the measure of objectivity in history will always differ from that in natural science. After all, historians traditionally have investigated all sorts of human matters charged with passion and emotion. By the very nature of the subject, history tends to divide scholars and to set them at odds. It is one thing to study pulleys and inclined planes, quite another the Second World War and the Holocaust. Moreover, the individual historians cannot always achieve detachment or indifference. Each one arguably displays a bias through the mere choice of a subject for study, perhaps the origin of a social problem, and then compounds the difficulty by bringing other partialities to it derived from culture, class, race, gender, religion, or some other form of personal identification. To be sure, affirmations of personal preference need not represent gross bigotries. Nevertheless, they may affect the value judgments in the narratives and all attempts at evaluation. Another problem resides in the historian's practice of choosing specific facts for inclusion, picking them from an already incomplete body of historical knowledge and thereby enhancing even more the chances of skewing the story in one way or another.

One appropriate response to such misgivings might suggest that, in fact, the dangers of writing history do not exceed appreciably those of natural science. Similar hazards exist in both areas. For example, natural scientists also choose a subject for investigation, such as cancer research, and perhaps in this way betray a bias acquired from life experiences. They also draw conclusions based on less-than-total knowledge. Indeed, no academic discipline aspires to recreate reality but rather to obtain some insight into its essential nature. For such reasons, the epistemological predicaments of natural science run parallel in important respects with those of history.

Nevertheless, historians do operate under a singular disadvantage. As American historian Carl L. Becker observed, "In truth the actual past is gone; and the world of history is an intangible world, re-created in our minds."[6] In contrast with many forms of natural science, no actual "object" ever comes under observation. Instead, using the remnants of the past, historians reconstruct history, employing statements of probability, not certainty, and subject always to the limitations of a point of view.

The angle of vision, or the point of view, renders historical narratives intelligible. Without them, historical artifacts would make no sense, and historical narratives would follow no coherent line of development. True, historians do not always agree, but different versions of the same events do not necessarily result in intellectual incompatibilities or error. Quite the contrary, divergent renditions may result in larger, complementary forms of understanding in which one enriches and animates the other from separate vantage points. Theoretically, no limits restrict the number of "true" stories historians can tell about the past. Charles Beard, an American historian, always maintained that his work, an economic interpretation of the United States Constitution, in no way nullified political or ideological or institutional treatments. It merely added a new dimension.

Though the difficulty of sorting through the problem of objectivity no doubt will remain a source of perplexity and consternation, historian Paul K. Conkin has suggested a wise way of moderating the dilemma. While properly refusing to abandon conceptions of truth and believability in historical narratives, he argued that somewhat different standards of objectivity must apply than in the natural sciences. Historians must adhere to their own rules of fairness, reason, and logic while constructing their stories about the human past. In addition, they must support their claims with some kind of actual evidence as the basis for plausible and valid inferences. To the extent that they comply, the works of historians will fulfill the requirements of objectivity.[7]

Historians can sacrifice conceptions of objectivity only at their own risk. A most disturbing manifestation has come about in recent times. A crowd of self-proclaimed "historical revisionists" has gained an audience by insisting that the genocide directed against European Jews during the Second World War never happened. These so-called "Holocaust deniers" depict claims of mass extermination as a gigantic hoax, perpetrated by Zionists in support of the state of Israel. Organized into "the Institute for Historical Review," they have published their denials in the *Journal of Historical Review*, a means of presentation dressed up with the appearance of scholarly apparatus in order to make untruths seem believable. According to historian Deborah Lipstadt, the leading authority on this phenomenon, such lies are the work of an unsavory group of pseudoscholars with pro-Nazi and anti-Semitic proclivities. None of them are professional historians. According to her powerful and distressing book, *Denying the Holocaust: The Growing Assault on Truth and Memory*, the reality of the Holocaust is not debatable.[8] The catastrophe happened, and the proof exists. Yet, gullible people in the United States and Europe have accepted the denial as plausible. Lipstadt calls upon historians as truth tellers to stand against this attempt at overturning reason and evidence. Epistemological integrity does count for something.

In conclusion, the discussion in this chapter aims at resolving none of the theoretical issues in dispute but rather at providing some guidance in following the main lines of debate and also at sounding an alert to some of the methodological pitfalls. Upon serious encounter, such issues allow for no facile assumptions about much of anything. The ongoing controversy over the "positivist" and "idealist" models have shaped the discussion but do not imply the existence of two different kinds of reality. Rather, they suggest two different attempts at comprehending portions of the natural and the historical worlds. They also recall the distinction established by Sir Isaiah Berlin in an essay on Leo Tolstoy's philosophy of history. Berlin derived his title, *The Hedgehog and the Fox*, from a line of poetry by Archilochus that said: "The fox knows many things, but the hedgehog knows one big thing."

Berlin believed that those words marked one of the deepest differences among writers and thinkers. As he explained in a kind of extended thesis statement:

> For there exists a great chasm between those, on the one side, who relate everything to a single central vision, one system less or more coherent or articulate, in terms of which they understand, think and feel—a single, universal, organizing principle in terms of which alone all that they are and say has significance—and, on the other side, those who pursue many ends, often unrelated and even contradictory, connected, if at all, only in some de facto way, for some psychological or physiological cause, related by no moral or aesthetic principle; these last lead lives, perform acts, and entertain ideas that are centrifugal rather than centripetal, their thought is scattered or diffused, moving on many levels, seizing upon the essence of a vast variety of experiences and objects for what they are in themselves without, consciously or unconsciously, seeking to fit them into or exclude them from, any one unchanging, all-embracing, sometimes self-contradictory and incomplete, at times fanatical, unitary inner vision.

In elaboration, he averred, "The first kind of intellectual and artistic personality belongs to the hedgehogs, the second to the foxes." Without insisting upon any kind of rigid classification, he suggested that Dante belonged to the first category, and Shakespeare to the second. Plato, Lucretius, Pascal, Hegel, Dostoevsky, Nietzsche, Ibsen, and Proust ranked as hedgehogs, and Herodotus, Aristotle, Montaigne, Erasmus, Moliere, Goethe, Pushkin, Balzac, and Joyce were foxes. His observations pointed toward something fundamental and widespread. If they held credence, then perhaps the very existence of the "positivist–idealist" dichotomy partook of the universal and expressed a distinctive facet of the workings of mind. If so, it may brook no resolution.[9]

## RECOMMENDED READINGS

Useful compilations are contained in Ronald H. Nash, ed., *Ideas of History*, Volume 2: *The Critical Philosophy of History* (New York: E. P. Dutton, 1969); Patrick Gardiner, ed., *Theories of History* (New York: The Free Press, 1959); and William H. Dray, ed., *Philosophical Analysis and History* (New York: Harper and Row, 1966). William H. Dray, *Philosophy of History*, 2nd ed. (Englewood Cliffs, NJ: Prentice-Hall, 1993); W. H. Walsh, *Philosophy of History: An Introduction*, rev. ed. (New York: Harper and Row, 1967); and the segment by Paul K. Conkin in Conkin and Roland N. Stromberg, *The Heritage and Challenge of History* (New York: Dodd, Mead and Company, 1971 ) provide additional materials. Conkin's thoughts on objectivity are contained in chapter ll. For a similar defense of conceptions of objectivity in history, see chapter 7 in Joyce Appleby, Lynn Hunt, and Margaret Jacob, *Telling the Truth about History* (New York: W. W. Norton, 1994). The main scholarly journal in this area is *History and Theory: Studies in the Philosophy of History*.

The debate over "the covering law" figures prominently in Arthur C. Danto, *Analytical Philosophy of History* (Cambridge, MA: At the University Press, 1965); William Dray, *Laws and Explanation in History* (New York: Oxford University Press, 1957); Haskell Fain, *Between Philosophy and History: The Resurrection of Speculative Philosophy of History within the Analytic Tradition* (Princeton, NJ: Princeton University Press, 1970); Leon J. Goldstein, *Historical Knowing* (Austin: University of Texas Press, 1976); Oscar Handlin, *Truth in History* (Cambridge, MA: Belknap Press of Harvard University Press, 1979); J. H. Hexter, *Doing History* (Bloomington: Indiana University Press, 1971); and Morton White, *Foundations of Historical Knowledge* (New York: Harper and Row, 1965). The two essays by Carl G. Hempel are reprinted in Nash and Gardiner. Representative writings by Carl Becker and Charles Beard are also in Nash. The emergence of an alternate view is examined by Georg G. Iggers, *The German Conception of History: The National Tradition of Historical Thought from Herder to the Present* (Middletown, CT: Wesleyan University Press, 1968). The premier statement of the "idealist" position, of course, is R. G. Collingwood, *The Idea of History* (New York: Oxford University Press, 1956). The concluding consideration comes from Isaiah Berlin, *The Hedgehog and the Fox* (New York: Mentor, 1957).

Important contributions to the literature include Robert William Fogel and G. R. Elton, *Which Road to the Past? Two Views of History* (New Haven: Yale University Press, 1983); and Peter Novick, *That Noble Dream: The "Objectivity Question"and the American Historical Profession* (New York: Cambridge University Press, 1988). John Tosh, *The Pursuit of History: Aims, Methods, and New Directions in the Study of Modern History*, 2nd ed. (London: Longman, 1991) covers many of the issues under review in this chapter. Deborah Lipstadt's *Denying the Holocaust: The Growing Assault on Truth and Memory* (New York: The Free Press, 1993) presents a dismaying account of a monstrous misuse of history.

## ENDNOTES

1.  Bruce Mazlish, *The Riddle of History: The Great Speculators from Vico to Freud* (New York: Minerva Press, 1966), 194–196.
2.  The foregoing comes from R. G. Collingwood, *The Idea of History* (New York: Oxford University Press, 1956), 204–215.
3.  Collingwood, *Idea of History*, 223.
4.  Ronald H. Nash, ed., *Ideas of History*, Vol. 2: *The Critical Philosophy of History* (New York: E. P. Dutton, 1969), 240.
5.  Carl G. Hempel, "The Function of General Laws in History," in *Theories of History*, ed. Patrick Gardiner (New York: The Free Press, 1959), 344, 348–349. First published in *The Journal of Philosophy*, 39 (15 January 1942): 36.
6.  Ronald H. Nash, ed., *Ideas of History*, Volume 2: *The Critical Philosophy of History* (New York: E. P. Dutton, 1969), 185.
7.  Paul K. Conkin and Roland N. Stromberg, *The Heritage and Challenge of History* (New York: Dodd, Mead and Company, 1971), 211; Joyce Appleby, Lynn Hunt, and Margaret Jacob, *Telling the Truth about History* (New York: W. W. Norton, 1994), chap. 7, also insists upon the importance of retaining conceptions of objectivity.
8.  Deborah Lipstadt, *Denying the Holocaust: The Growing Assault on Truth and Memory* (New York: The Free Press, 1993).
9.  Isaiah Berlin, *The Hedgehog and the Fox: An Essay on Tolstoy's View of History* (New York: Mentor, 1957), 7–8.

# 6

# *Reading, Writing, and Research*

For students of history, no matter whether novices or professionals, the responsibilities of reading, writing, and research hold special importance. As consumers and producers of scholarship, historians need to cultivate some particular kinds of skills. The reading requires certain powers of retention and synthesis, a capacity to work over large bodies of information and to establish a measure of intellectual possession. The writing calls for an ability to communicate clearly, in the case of history, in plain, jargon-free prose; and the research compels, among other things, orderly, systematic, and imaginative forms of inquiry. The degree to which students of history can attain such capabilities will determine their successes and failures.

Historical writing falls into several categories. The textbook, the most pervasive on college campuses, contains general introductory accounts. It functions as a place to begin and as a sort of reference work. Other categories include narrowly conceived scholarly articles and monographs, broader synthetic works, and doctoral dissertations. Each has a standard format and a particular role to play. Within the guild of historians, such types of writing bear the descriptive name "secondary source." They are "secondary" in that historians have derived them from "primary sources," that is, documentary materials in archives and other forms of artifact.

Doctoral dissertations serve as launch pads for aspiring scholars. They come into being as a concluding experience at the end of graduate school and mark the advent of a professional career. In most cases, they focus on a small, even minuscule, topic, possibly something like the politics of the Whig party in Massachusetts during the war with Mexico. They almost always show the effects of pressure and deadlines. Among other things, they demonstrate a capacity to carry out research in primary sources and to write up the findings intelligibly. Completed dissertations affirm credentials of a sort but have never won over large audiences. For a variety of reasons, the readership has remained small and elite, mainly consisting of the faculty examining committee and perhaps members of the immediate family.

Doctoral dissertations often turn into scholarly articles and monographs. Such outlets make possible the dissemination of specialized research, addressed primarily to professional scholars. Periodicals such as *The Journal of American History* and *The American Historical Review,* among the most prestigious in the United States, publish essays of wide interest to historians generally, while others, such as *Diplomatic History* or *The Annals of Iowa,* center on themes and regions. A unique journal of some kind provides for discussion of practically every subfield. Consider as examples *Forest History, The Hispanic American Historical Review,* and *The Journal of Negro History.* Scholarly monographs, in contrast, usually appear as books and also aim principally at other professional historians. Characteristically based on extensive work in archives, they explore a narrow subject in substantial detail and often argue an explicit thesis. In other words, they present the research findings within the context of a particular line of reasoning. Such publications have titles such as *Pan American Visions: Woodrow Wilson in the Western Hemisphere, 1913–1921,* or *The Great Anatolian Rebellion, 1000–1020/1591–1611.* They also have comparatively small audiences.

Synthetic works in history often project more ambitious goals. Usually an outgrowth of the author's own specialized labors in the field, this kind of book also draws extensively on the research of others and seeks to portray the subject under discussion in broad and accessible terms. Such works invite the attention of intelligent lay readers. As works of synthesis, these publications investigate a period or pursue a theme while drawing on the whole body of pertinent scholarship in order to develop an interpretation. They have titles such as *Europe and the French Imperium, 1799–1814* or *In the Shadow of FDR: From Harry Truman to Ronald Reagan.*

Formal writing by students consists at least of three types. These include the interpretive essay, the book review, and the research paper. Though specifications will vary, depending on the wishes of individual instructors, some general pointers may serve a useful purpose. Again, the object is suggestive, not prescriptive. Some additional hints on clear writing will follow.

The interpretive essay calls for a reasoned response to a question of some sort, presented always with proper regard for the rules of logic and evidence. The exercise may take place in class as an essay examination or outside as a take-home project. In either instance, the fundamental expectation remains much the same. The student needs to develop a coherent and defensible line of thinking. The wise instructor probably will place less value upon encyclopedic but uncritical answers than upon those essays characterized by analysis, generalization, and evaluation. Critical thinking, after all, is the point.

Most kinds of formal writing should begin with some sort of thesis statement. It affirms the main theme under consideration and provides an indication of how the narrative will unfold. The first paragraph of an interpretive essay should assert the thesis and then the ensuing segments should set forth the reasoning and the evidence. Suppose the question asked for a discussion of the extent to which U. S. imperial expansion at the turn of the twentieth century conformed with the Marxist-Leninist explanation. Any conceivable answer would have to presume some knowledge of Marxism-Leninism; the thesis statement would set forth a claim either in favor of the proposition or against it, and then the main body of the presentation would round out the argument with specifics, details, examples, illustrations, and the like. Critical analysis should run throughout, and at the end a conclusion should reaffirm the point of the thesis, now regarded as a working hypothesis vindicated by the preceding analysis.

A book review calls for an appraisal of a work published by a practicing writer. Readily accessible examples in history abound in scholarly journals, such as *The American Historical Review* or *The Journal of American History*. Though professional historians often dash off book reviews routinely, such projects pose special problems for beginning students who lack experience and familiarity with the other literature on the subject. At the minimum, this kind of writing should accomplish two aims. It should describe the contents of the book and also develop a critical appraisal.

When picking a book to review, students should choose something based on their own special interests, assuming of course that they have been given some range of choice. As they proceed through the volume, they should take brief reading notes, recording the main points and themes of each chapter. This practice will help them in keeping track of the discussion and also will assist them in the writing. As a flexible rule of thumb, about one page of review for each one hundred pages of text should suffice. A full bibliographical citation should adorn the top of the page, followed by the commentary, presented in proper, idiomatic language with an appropriate regard for the rules of grammar and the conventions of style.

Book reviews ordinarily incorporate two parts. The first provides a synthesis of the contents, conveying some idea of the book's subject and the author's manner of addressing it. The second sets forth a critical evaluation and asks most essentially whether the book articulates believable, verifiable, and legitimate claims. In arriving at such judgments, the book reviewer needs to ask at least three additional questions. Are the lines of argument logical, coherent, and consistent? Does the evidence presented allow just grounds for making the inferences? Does the author have appropriate qualifications for writing such a book? In other words, the reviewer must look out for signs of bias, prejudice, distortion, and misrepresentation and then arrive at an appraisal accordingly. To mention some egregious examples, a work on race relations in the United States by a member of the Ku Klux Klan probably would arouse suspicion; so would a history of the Standard Oil Company by a vulgar Marxist, a study of the spread of Christianity by a fierce atheist, or an investigation into the historical effects of gun control by a member of the National Rifle Association. Good professional scholarship should not incorporate blatant forms of bigotry and unreason.

The research paper, a stern and demanding test, often elicits a panicked response. Sometimes seen in student circles as a form of cruel and unusual punishment of dubious constitutional standing, the chance to engage independently in research also holds forth opportunities, as long as students proceed under suitable guidance and with some sense for the proper and feasible. Adherence to the following precautions should ease the emotional trauma and enhance the chance of taking part in an intellectual experience. Indeed, with genuine care and planning, some measure of personal satisfaction might even result.

First and foremost, the selection of a topic holds critical importance. Many students doom their own efforts at the outset through the choice of a hopelessly dull or unrealistic topic. For most undergraduates, a treatise on the origin of street names in Odell, Texas, would not hold much promise. Also, students need to calculate whether they possess the appropriate library resources, the necessary specialized knowledge and skills, and the capacity to cover the subject adequately within the allowable space and time. Aspiring researchers should shy away from subjects such as "French Military Debacles since Napoleon" if they have no access to French works on military history, no knowledge of the French language, and no more than fifteen pages in which to carry out the assignment. As a general rule, students should assume that if they can define and circumscribe their subjects with some precision, they will acquire an advantage. In other words, they need to establish rules of inclusion and exclusion and to center their efforts when possible on a unified theme or purpose. Imagination always figures prominently by giving vitality to the enterprise.

Once having chosen a workable topic, the novice scholar next needs to mount a systematic search for research materials. In the old days, before libraries went to computers, the card catalog was one place to begin; it listed the holdings of a particular library. A more demanding and effective procedure, providing access to the whole literature, required consultation with other bibliographical guides and aides. Examples might include the *International Index to Periodicals*, the *Readers' Guide to Periodical Literature*, the *Handbook of Latin American Studies*, the *Harvard Guide to American History*, and the *Guide to American Foreign Relations since 1700*. Many other such bibliographical tools exist, and reference librarians, of course, can provide indispensable help.

Many such bibliographical guides and aids now have become available in computerized formats. Research libraries have adopted on-line catalogs that perform the function of card catalogs faster and in many instances more efficiently. They too facilitate the location of research materials by means of author, title, and subject. By entering a few well-chosen words into the terminal, researchers can obtain long lists of pertinent books, articles, and even manuscript collections. In addition, the catalogs of major research libraries are accessible through computers linked in regional, national, and international on-line networks. Making a trip to the Library of Congress in Washington, D.C., by electronic means can instill a sense of awe even in hardened researchers.

Other computer adaptations include dial-up services such as Dialog, search engines such as Yahoo and Lycos, and CD-ROM–based systems. Such databases allow access to thousands of informational sites and bibliographical indexes, organized much like the old-fashioned card catalog by author, title, and subject. They also allow for searches by key words. Such advances, while unquestionably marvelous technologically, also compel some measure of caution. Students, for example, should know that some computerized library catalogs may list the holdings of only the past twenty or twenty-five years, although to be sure the number grows smaller all the time. Also, some reference-book databases are selective and may exclude publications essential to a specific historical topic, and the findings determined by search engines will depend upon the instructions of the user. Anyone conducting a bibliographical search on a computer must select the key words for entry very carefully or run the risk of adverse consequences. According to one horror story, perhaps apocryphal, a zoologist seeking information on how to move anaesthetized grizzly bears from one wilderness habitat to another entered the words "bears" and "drugged" into the computer and wound up with five articles on the legal misadventures of professional athletes, notably, Chicago Bears from the National Football League. Such hazards bear thinking about. But in spite of them, the computer as a "defining technology" recalling the mechanical clock and the steam engine has altered significantly how historians do their work. For fuller discussion of such things, Janice L. Reiff's *Structuring the Past: The Uses of Computers in History* and Daniel I. Greenstein, *A Historian's Guide to Computing*, provide introductions.

The efficient conduct of research in any academic discipline requires systemic, orderly, and disciplined habits. Two inviolable rules underscore the point and also the need for accuracy. First, always obtain complete bibliographical citations for all sources and record them in the old-fashioned way on 3 × 5 index cards for the files or in the computer. Incomplete or erroneous information will always cause subsequent difficulties and delays. Second, take usable research notes, always indicating the location of the source and the pages from which the information comes. In the transcription, ordinarily only one idea should go on any single note, and paraphrasing usually has more utility than direct quotation. The former practice facilitates the task of putting the material into one's own words. If a quote has special charm, then absolute accuracy must be used to retain and cite it.

The mechanical process of taking notes can assume several forms. In the old days before computers, some researchers liked to write their findings in loose-leaf notebooks, dividing carefully the various entries so that later they could tear them into strips and organize them topically and chronologically for the writing. Another approach employed the use of 5× 7 cards for easy shuffling. In recent times, word-processing techniques have become popular, enabling researchers with notebook computers to go into libraries and archives and assemble their own databases. In any case, no matter what the method, the need for systematic, orderly, and accurate thoroughness retains a vital importance. To make the point another way, the researcher must carry out each task with painstaking completeness and should do it the same way every time.

While writing a research paper, the appropriate techniques for citing sources and invoking authorities have always given students problems. Whether to employ footnotes or endnotes often depends upon the instructor's preferences. Recent tendencies favor endnotes. No matter which method is used, the writer must make certain judgments about inclusion and exclusion—that is, what information to put in the notes and what not. As a rule of thumb, authors can safely assume that if an ordinary textbook on the subject would contain a certain piece of information, no need exists to verify it in a note. On the other hand, if a well-informed reader might not know, then a note should appear in order to provide appropriate direction to the source. Footnotes and endnotes enable readers to follow the writer's research methods. In addition, the rules of scholarship also require the attribution of direct quotations and extended paraphrases. Scholars need to indicate where the words and thoughts came from. Otherwise, they run the risk of plagiarism, one of the worst of academic crimes. Plagiarism, simply defined, consists of taking someone else's words or ideas and passing them off as one's own without giving proper credit. It amounts to stealing.

The actual writing should follow the rules and conventions of grammar and style and can achieve good results through the exercise of care, practice, patience, and careful editing. The latter function has become comparatively easy with the adoption of word-processing techniques on computers. According to Janice L. Reiff, word processing thus far has had the most significant effect on how historians and their students do their work. The most important hallmarks of effective historical writing consist of clarity, precision, and accessibility. In most cases, historians seek to write their narratives in plain language and to convey their thoughts exactly enough so that all interested readers can obtain the means of entry. The following suggestions, while hardly exhaustive, may provide some guidance.

First, the structure and organization of formal writing require planning and restraint. Reliance on metaphorical language, the free association of ideas, or other such devices have an important place in some kinds of literature but normally not in history. In this field, pointedness, simplicity, and directness establish the means of communication. Another characteristic features a compelling logical flow to move the reader readily from one point to the next.

Sentences and paragraphs make up the building blocks. Sentences contain at least a subject and a verb. The rules of formal writing forbid the use of any construction other than a complete sentence. Paragraphs begin with a topic sentence and articulate a single thought or a closely related group of thoughts. At the end, a transitional sentence should facilitate the movement from one paragraph to the next. Throughout, logic and reason should keep similar subjects and themes in close proximity.

Second, effective formal writing compels close adherence to the rules of grammar and the conventions of style. At bare minimum, this injunction means that subjects and verbs agree, that correct punctuation separate the various units of composition, that the consistent use of capital letters designate some proper nouns, that apostrophes indicate possession, and that ambiguous antecedents never appear. Large measures of confusion and ignorance surround such matters, compounded often by a cavalier attitude. Modern-day philistines pay little heed, demeaning the role of the capital, dismissing the apostrophe, and treating commas, periods, colons, semicolons, dashes, and hyphens as interchangeable. Such lawless and disrespectful practices run many risks, including the loss of communicative skills. Happily, reliance on any good English grammar book can provide the remedy.

Questions of style depend less upon rules than upon the dictates of good taste. They impinge upon a variety of concerns. For example, beginning writers should rely primarily on short, declarative sentences. To be sure, writers need to vary the structure and the rhythm, but they should never affect grandiloquence and never employ turgid, complex, pompous, or bombastic constructions. To express themselves in positive form, they should present the main thought conspicuously in the main clause without undue embellishment and then let it go. A related concern focuses on excessive verbiage. To make the point in command form, eschew wordiness. Never use more words than necessary.

In a masterful little book, *The Elements of Style*, authors William Strunk, Jr., and E. B. White set forth good advice with these words:

> Vigorous writing is concise. A sentence should contain no unnecessary words, a paragraph no unnecessary sentences, for the same reason that a drawing should have no unnecessary lines and a machine no unnecessary parts. This requires not that the writer make all his sentences short, or that he avoid all detail and treat his subjects only in outline, but that every word tell.[2]

Violations take place in the use of phrases such as "the question as to whether," "there is no doubt but that," "she is a woman who," and "this is a subject that."

Tense, voice, and verb selection also have importance. In most cases in historical writing, the simple past tense is most appropriate. By and large, inexperienced writers should favor the active voice more than the passive voice. This distinction emphasizes the importance of employing strong verbs. In the first, the subject acts upon the object directly and yields a lean, muscular sentence. "During visits to Washington, Colonel House influenced President Wilson's conduct of international statecraft." The following, in contrast, produces a backward and clumsy sentence in which the object acts upon the verb. "In the conduct of international statecraft, President Wilson was influenced by Colonel House during his visits to Washington." A particularly annoying example of a passive-voice construction asserts, "The first trip to Boston will always be remembered by me."

Responsible students should avoid such abominations, unless perhaps they aspire to careers in bureaucracy, government, university administration, and certain aspects of law and insurance, in which cases studied ambiguity and indirection often take on some measure of utility. Press secretaries for any high official could not dispense with phrases such as "it has been decided" or "it will be determined." These passive-voice constructions present masterpieces of evasion, disallowing any attempt to fix responsibility. In contrast, the careful writer concerned with clarity will stick with strong, active verbs.

Skilled writers try to stay away from jargon, cliches, and euphemisms. To be sure, some kinds of subjects require the use of technical terms, but generally the principle still holds in favor of simple language. Some examples will illustrate the nature of the problem. After participating in a briefing at large state university, an Air Force general actually expressed gratitude for the opportunity "to interface" with his audience. Computer terminology in this instance poses a threat. Similar fancy renditions might describe two professors talking as taking part in "information transfer." Clarity remains the aim. During the Watergate scandal in the 1970s, when President Nixon's press secretary, Ron Ziegler, characterized certain statements as "inoperative," he meant that they were false. Later, when President Carter referred to the attempted rescue mission of the hostages in Iran as "an incomplete success," he implied that it had failed. In the late 1990s, President Bill Clinton's tortured use of legal language to deny a sexual relationship with Monica Lewinski produced laughter, disbelief, and outrage among his listeners. Considerations of proper usage also forbid the employment of words ending in "ize," such as "maximize" or "prioritize," and the omnipresent "hopefully."

The following mangled sentences illustrate some additional errors to avoid. Though unintentionally comic in effect, they represent serious lapses of a most debilitating sort and demonstrate the need always to edit carefully.

### *Words Out of Proper Proximity*

"I saw a woman covered with blood holding her head in her hands."

"Babies have been known to hiccough before they are born. An unborn child has been heard as far as 25 feet away from its mother."

"Four Indian tribes are selling liquor on the reservation they purchased from out-of-state wholesalers."

"When diagnosed as a victim of acquired immune deficiency syndrome, the patient threatened to commit suicide rather than die."

"The robber was described as a six-foot-tall man with a mustache weighing 150 pounds."

"The exiles closely watched the overhead monitors, wondering whether the plane would be late again and sipping Cuban coffee."

"Victor Parker has the title role in 'Medea,' a 1948 adaption of Euripides' play about betrayal and revenge at Portland State University."

"Lloyd Hand is the son of a Danish sea captain who had to quit school at 13 when his father died to go to work."

"Late-night viewers were surprised to see Johnny Carson show up following his recent vacation with a beard."

### The Double Negative

"Type A behavior frequently begins very early in childhood because inadequate amounts of unconditional love and affection are not given to youngsters by both of their parents."

"When chided by his schoolteacher daughter about his poor use of English, the Texas millionaire oilman replied, 'Sallie, good grammar never made me no dollars.'"

### The Mixed Metaphor

"In several recently published studies, the importance of the disciplines in the arts, humanities, and social sciences has been recognized as pivotal in the academic fabric of the university."

### Foreign Terms Misused

"The musical program featured a sixteen-voice acapulco choir."

"Hord'derves of selected seafood items are included with all dinners."

"After shooting down nine Japanese planes over the Pacific, the fighter pilot was proclaimed a bonified World War II ace."

### Bureaucratic Gibberish

"There have been several students come in and reduce their work-study awards this semester. With this extra money, I may be able to increase the allocation of students in your department that are running out of funds. There is no restriction on type of work-study, either need or merit, but I must be able to fit the increased award into the student's financial aid budget. Have your students that may be running out of money come and see me. Hopefully I can help them finish the school year on work-study and save you money."

"Using the following information regarding temperamental traits would you please write a detail description of your child's temperament. Your child did this exercise in class regarding how they view their own temperament. Our hope is that you as a parent will share, honestly, your view of their temperament. In order for your child to receive credit for this assignment they must turn in a signed copy of your assessment. Hopefully this will be an enlightening experience."

Such grammatical and stylistic atrocities provide just cause for thoughtfulness and restraint and call forth sober responses from both amateurs and professionals.

The process of composition and publication by professional historians takes place at the conclusion of extended efforts. For most, the research experience, alternately wearying and exhilarating, concentrates work in the "primary" sources. They come in various kinds. Some appear as documentary collections in published form, others as reproductions on microfilm or microcards, and many in archives and libraries as original manuscripts. The conduct of research sometimes requires travel to many locations, surely a significant fringe benefit. Knowing the location of collections and the means of access thus takes on substantial importance.

Published documents provide historians with a place to begin. Many governments more or less systematically print collections of documents, proceedings, and state papers. To an extent, these endeavors fulfill a propaganda purpose and establish "official" versions of events. Significant series such as the *Papers Relating to the Foreign Relations of the United States* and the *Congressional Record* serve the interests of historians but sometimes induce a kind of adversarial relationship. Scholars have a vested stake in openness and accessibility of information, while officials typically put less stock in making public the whole truth. Another kind of published primary source consists of the personal papers of influential people, such as Thomas Jefferson, Theodore Roosevelt, or Booker T. Washington. Usually put out by university presses, these expensive and ambitious undertakings make available vital research material and usually exist among the holdings of good libraries.

Reproductions of microfilm and microcards, in contrast, make possible the dissemination of historical records at relatively low cost. Though sometimes cumbersome and annoying to use, such devices reduce travel costs and make possible the working through of documentary collections while staying at home with a mechanical reader. These efforts serve commendable purposes. The National Archives of the United States has benefited the community of scholars in all sorts of ways by facilitating a host of microfilm collections, comprising many of the records of the Departments of State, War, Navy, Treasury, Justice, and Interior. In the future, documentary sources made available by electronic means through the use of computers may further change the way historians do their work.

Manuscript collections constitute the raw material from which historians fashion their narratives, and they have a fixed location. The actual sites range from college libraries to local and regional historical societies to official governmental archives at all levels to presidential libraries. Most grant access to qualified researchers without undue harassment but also maintain security precautions against theft. In the Library of Congress and the National Archives in Washington, D.C., armed guards scrutinize the scholars at work and routinely search briefcases and book bags. Classification restrictions also present hazards for historians interested in the very recent past. The right to know does not always apply, especially in delicate areas concerning military and diplomatic affairs. Governments in England and Western Europe by and large adhere to a fifty-year rule, allowing the records to become available after the passage of time. In the United States, the authorities traditionally have tried to achieve declassification more rapidly but always have problems in obtaining the goal.

The actual contents of archival collections consist of the original correspondence, memoranda, and diary entries exchanged and recorded by the historical actors. All such artifacts require special care and handling. The major repositories in the United States include the National Archives, the Library of Congress, and the various presidential libraries. The first contains the records of federal agencies; the second, the collected personal papers of notable people; and the third, research materials on all of the presidencies since Herbert Hoover. The decentralization of archival resources in presidential libraries has caused logistical problems for scholars who need to travel about from one to another; nevertheless, it has become the standard practice. Archival research in foreign countries affords special opportunities and hazards. Differences in language, culture, and custom all create potential impediments; yet, for many historians, the conduct of research in another country ranks among the most challenging and enriching of experiences. More often than not, the joys of pursuing the hunt provide compensation for the frustrations.

The foregoing discussion may suggest to some readers that an undergraduate experience with history ought properly to result in the professional practice of history. Such, of course, is not the case. The vast majority of history majors never become professors. Quite the contrary, they pursue an immense diversity of professions. Quite literally, they do everything under the sun, developing careers in teaching, law, the ministry, the military, business, government, and other such areas. Limited only by the extent of their own imaginations, they possess many transferable skills and can do many different things.

As students of the liberal arts, history majors possess many capabilities of which they are sometimes insufficiently aware. If they have cultivated their talents properly, they should emerge from their colleges and universities with a capacity to write and speak well, to think critically, to carry out research, and to make judgments about large and confusing masses of information. The attainment of literacy, always a laudable goal, should serve them well in all fields of endeavor. The ability to articulate thoughts clearly and to interpret them correctly will always establish an edge.

Though vocationalism and an obsessional concern for getting a job have pervaded higher education in the United States in recent times, those disciplines making up the liberal arts have played their traditional role by upholding the importance of creativity, understanding, and communication. Without them, nothing much can function properly. Various studies now suggest that the average twenty-one-year-old will switch careers no less than three times in a working lifetime. This prediction, even if only approximately true, should reaffirm the viability of the liberal arts as a means of achieving adaptability. The knowledge never becomes obsolete. The following skills inventory underscores the point by heightening a sense of awareness. Though presented as a practical aid in obtaining employment, it also shows some of the advantages derived from some exposure to the disciplines in the liberal arts.

## SKILLS INVENTORY*

Before you begin the interviewing process connected with a job hunt, it is important that you develop a strong knowledge base of your qualifications. Over the years, you have developed many transferable skills from coursework, extracurricular activities, and your total life experiences. If you've researched topics and written, edited, and presented a paper for a history class, you've used transferable skills. Your planning and coordinating of a spring banquet used transferables. These skills are not limited to any one academic discipline or knowledge area. They are found in courses and other experiences that are broadly applicable to many occupational areas. Students who can describe their skills to a prospective employer will present themselves as those who know how to apply their liberal education to a work environment.

### The Skills Checklist

On the next three pages is a list of broad skill areas that are developed in a liberal arts college. Below the general heading is a breakdown of more specific skills:

### Instructions

1. Review the list and check (√) those skills you feel you possess.
2. Review those skills you checked. In the column next to the checklist, mark your skills with a rating to indicate your ability in each area:
   1 = enough ability to get by, with help from others
   2 = some ability
   3 = definite, strong ability in this area
3. In the fourth column, "Evidence," record examples of situations and specific results that support your selections of skills you see

---

*Courtesy of Career Development Center, Gustavus Adolphus College.

as being rated "2" or "3"—for example, if you checked "Motivating," record the specific situation: "Teaching older women to swim involved constant motivation and encouragement."

There are likely many more skills than are listed on this worksheet. Explore your personal experiences in work, school, and your social environment. Be sure to record any additional skills you have developed.

| SKILLS INVENTORY | | |
| --- | --- | --- |
| Skill | Rating 1—3 | Evidence |
| **Communication:** The skillful expression, transmission, and interpretation of knowledge and ideas. | | COMMUNICATION: |
| Effective Speaking | | |
| Concise Writing | | |
| Attentive Listening | | |
| Expression of Ideas | | |
| Facilitating Group Discussion | | |
| Appropriate Feedback | | |
| Negotiating | | |
| Perceiving Nonverbal Messages | | |
| Persuading | | |
| Reporting of Information | | |
| Describing Feelings | | |
| Interviewing | | |
| Editing | | |
| **Research and Planning:** The search for specific knowledge and the ability to conceptualize the future and create the process for getting there. | | RESEARCH AND PLANNING: |
| Forecast, Predict | | |
| Creative Ideas | | |
| Identification of Problem | | |
| Imagine Alternatives | | |

*(Continued)*

| SKILLS INVENTORY (Continued) | | |
|---|---|---|
| Skill | Rating 1—3 | Evidence |
| Identification of Resources | | |
| Gathering Information | | |
| Problem Solving | | |
| Goal Setting | | |
| Extracting Important Information | | |
| Defining Needs | | |
| Analyzing | | |
| Developing Evaluation Strategy | | |
| **Human Relations Skills:** The use of interpersonal skills for resolving conflict and relating to and helping people. | | HUMAN RELATIONS SKILLS: |
| Developing Rapport | | |
| Sensitivity | | |
| Listening | | |
| Conveying Feelings | | |
| Drawing Out People | | |
| Motivating | | |
| Sharing Credit | | |
| Counseling | | |
| Cooperation | | |
| Delegating with Respect for Others | | |
| Representing Others | | |
| Perception of Feelings, Situations | | |
| Assertiveness | | |
| Additional Skills: | | |
| **Organization, Management, or Leadership:** The ability to supervise, direct, and guide individuals and groups in the completion of tasks and fulfillment of goals. | | ORGANIZATION MANAGEMENT, OR LEADERSHIP: |
| Initiating New Ideas | | |
| Handling Details | | |

*(Continued)*

| SKILLS INVENTORY (Continued) | | |
|---|---|---|
| Skill | Rating 1—3 | Evidence |
| Decision Making | | |
| Coordinating Tasks | | |
| Managing Groups | | |
| Delegating Responsibility | | |
| Teaching | | |
| Coaching | | |
| Counseling | | |
| Promoting Change | | |
| Selling an Idea | | |
| Decision Making with Others | | |
| Conflict Management | | |
| Additional Skills: | | |

## RECOMMENDED READINGS

Useful manuals on style and method abound. *The Modern Researcher*, 5th ed. (New York: Harcourt Brace Jovanovich, 1992) by Jacques Barzun and Henry Graff ranks as a classic. Other references include *Historians and the Living Past: The Theory and Practice of Historical Study* (Arlington Heights, IL: AHM Publishing Corporation, 1978) by Allan J. Lichtman and Valerie French; *Understanding History: A Primer of Historical Method*, 2nd ed. (New York: Alfred A. Knopf, 1969) by Louis Gottschalk; *A Guide to Historical Method* (Homewood, IL: The Dorsey Press, 1969) ed. Robert Jones Shafer; *Creative History*, 2nd ed. (Philadelphia: J. B. Lippincott Company, 1973) by W. T. K. Nugent; *Historian's Handbook: A Key to the Study and Writings of History*, 2nd ed. (Boston: Houghton Mifflin Company, 1964) by Wood Gray and others; and *Studying History: An Introduction to Methods and Structure*, 3rd ed. (Washington, DC: American Historical Association, 1985) by Paul L. Ward. Writing techniques and other issues come under consideration in *A Manual of Style*, 14th ed. (Chicago: The University of Chicago Press, 1993); *Harbrace College Handbook*, 9th ed. (New York: Harcourt Brace Jovanovich, 1982) by John C. Hodges and Mary E. Whitten; *Writer's Guide: History* (Lexington, MA: D. C. Heath, 1987; *A Pocket Style Manual* (Boston: Bedford Books, 1993); and *The Elements of Style*, 3rd ed. (New York: Macmillan, 1979) by William Strunk, Jr., and E. B. White.

James Kilpatrick's former column "On Writing" in the Gannett news-papers provided some atrocious examples. On computing, Bryan Pfaffen-berger, *The Scholar's Personal Computing Handbook: A Practical Guide* (Boston: Little, Brown and Company, 1986); and Janice L. Reiff, *Structuring the Past: The Uses of Computers in History* (Washington, DC: American Historical Association, 1991); and Daniel I. Greenstein, *A Historian's Guide to Computing* (New York: Oxford University Press, 1994) are places to begin. Contemporary book-stores are bulging with computer manuals. Professor James E. Hansen III at Colorado State University also shared his expertise.

## ENDNOTES

1. Professor James E. Hansen III at Colorado State University provided me with this anecdote.
2. William Strunk, Jr., and E. B. White, *The Elements of Style,* 3rd ed. (New York: Macmillan Publishing Company, 1979), 23.

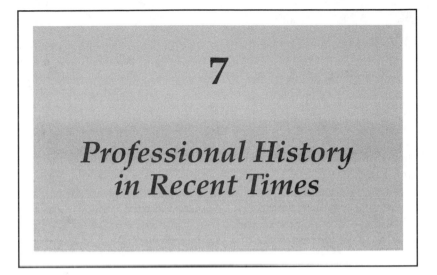

# 7

# *Professional History in Recent Times*

The professionalization of history in the middle of the nineteenth century produced profound changes in focus and direction; it also inspired fierce struggles over purposes and methods. When historians first endorsed a conception of "scientific" history, they tried to promote the detached and "objective" examination of documentary evidence in order to obtain irrefutable truths about the past. They emphasized the utilization of assiduous research and stringent techniques. Their successors in later years placed less credibility in such simple, naive faiths. Some doubted the accessibility of unquestionable verities and urged instead the acquisition of socially useful insights, emphasizing the importance of the relative angle from which historians viewed their subjects. Others, seeking more inclusive and reliable methods, hoped to possess deeper levels of understanding by extending the bounds of inquiry beyond the political, military, and diplomatic activities of male elites and through the application of the social sciences. The ensuing endeavors had mixed results. Though historical studies became more precise and thorough, the preoccupations of professionalization also resulted in isolation and fragmentation. As a consequence of rampant specialization, common varieties of historical understanding broke down; in their place, pluralistic interpretations gave testimony to the disparities of human experience.

The outcomes reflected the very nature of recent times. In an important work entitled *Historiography: Ancient, Medieval and Modern,* historian Ernst Breisach argues that four characteristics of modern history particularly affected historical thinking in the years after 1870. These consisted of the impact of natural science, the process of industrialization, the emergence of mass culture, and shifting perceptions of the global world. According to this view, science, often regarded as the model of all knowledge, set profound epistemological problems before historians. Meanwhile, the disruptions brought about by the Industrial Revolution destroyed traditional understanding of cultural unity and historical continuity. In similar fashion, the emergence of mass movements, the concentration of populations in urban regions, and ensuing radical political appeals among the people directed attention to life among the common folk, while the triumph of the West over much of the remainder of the globe gave credence to certain Eurocentric ideas of world history. In combination, the effects shattered uniform pictures of the past and resulted in great divergences.

During the closing years of the nineteenth century, the so-called "hard" sciences acquired immense prestige for their supposed capacities to produce demonstrable claims about reality and to develop reliable predictive devices. Because such presumed certainties possessed irresistible appeal, students of human affairs, including historians, looked toward them as examples to emulate. But the effort collided with enormous conceptual difficulties, chief among them the distinction between the general and the particular. Though of course not always the case, the sciences characteristically developed general statements about the natural world, while history concentrated on particularistic statements about human affairs. If historians should substitute a concern for the common and the repeatable for the singular and the unique, their discipline might lose identity altogether. If universal principles and covering-law theories should become the objects of their search, then history would have to undergo a transformation in the image of physics or chemistry or else would cease to exist as a legitimate form of knowledge.

The epistemological controversies already reviewed in an earlier chapter pitted positivists against idealists and sometimes set historians against one another. Though innovators in response invoked the social sciences in the quest for methodological reassurance and scientific exactitude, traditionalists resisted the allure of arguments by analogy, insisting that in their field the term *science* possessed a more restricted meaning. For them, methodological rigor required that they strip away unwarranted theological and philosophical assumptions, accumulate the evidence, and then scrutinize it coldly, analytically, and objectively without preconceptions. Once understood in appropriate detail and with the necessary degree of detachment, history, as English historian J. B. Bury observed in 1903, would amount to a science, "no less and no more."[1]

Other historians, spurred on by the harsh, unrelenting circumstances of the industrial age, arrived at new understandings of the "true" forces shaping history. For them, in an era of dramatic and jolting economic change, abstract and idealistic conceptions of the universe, no matter whether defined in supernatural or metaphysical or rationalistic terms, held less reality than the press of material conditions. According to the materialistic view, the actual world consisted of economic struggle to obtain a livelihood, and the pursuit of wealth functioned as a prime determinant of human behavior. Karl Marx set forth his positions on these subjects in the middle of the nineteenth century, and henceforth, subsequent renditions, both of the Marxist and non-Marxist varieties, directed attention toward the organization of the productive system and the means by which people earned their living. Such pursuits turned into economic history.

The concentration of burgeoning urban masses in the cities also compelled notice and contributed to new kinds of social history. They focused on common, ordinary people. Though never completely anonymous in historical narratives, such persons, typically powerless, inconspicuous, and caught up in the cycles of birth, labor, and death, normally took subordinate places to the dominant ruling male elites who controlled politics, diplomacy, and war. Indeed, the very historical records employed by historians—political, diplomatic, and military—restricted access to the lesser folk. They showed up mainly in the announcements of birth and death. Though Marxist analyses emphasized the reality of the class struggle throughout, most nineteenth-century historians who wrote about "the people" had in mind collectivities of human beings who together found their stories incorporated into the histories of their nations. In the twentieth century, in contrast, historians turned their investigations to the development of group identities, particularly workers, peasants, racial and ethnic groups, women, and families. Within such categories, the main historical actors oftentimes could not find their stories within the traditional, national histories, and they demanded new ones.

Finally, the Western ascendancy over much of the rest of the world compelled self-congratulatory conceptions of universal or world history. Almost always ethnocentric, the various renditions, whether providential or secular, Christian or Marxist, characteristically took Europe as the model of historical development for all of humanity and displayed little sensitivity to the experiences of other peoples in other cultures. Oswald Spengler, of course, ranked as a notable exception. In such interpretive schemes, differences appeared as deviances, and European standards became the norms, indeed, the very hallmarks of civilization itself. In the nineteenth century, imperial triumphs in Asia, Africa, and the Middle East impressed Europeans not only as manifestations of a divinely ordained, civilizing mission in the barbarous regions but as irrefutable signs of their own intrinsic superiority, defined in Darwinian terms as justification for ascendancy over the lesser breeds. In the United States, an ideological counterpart affirmed the doctrines of manifest destiny. Under the impact of such deceits, universal or world history became merely a projection of the European (or North American) experience, part and parcel of the progressive thrust moving the inhabitants of the globe ever onward. In recent times, certain sociological and economic theories of "modernization" based on Western models, for example, W. W. Rostow's *The Stages of Economic Growth: A Non-Communist Manifesto* (1960), incorporated vestiges of the theme, but for the most part in much of the rest of the world, such ideas lost credibility after 1945, when the Europeans lost their dominance and their empires. As a consequence, Western scholars with a serious interest in non-Western history had to start all over again, seeking out new categories and means of analysis by which to make comprehensible the histories of non-European peoples on their own terms.

At the end of the nineteenth century, European historians took a special interest in the continuities of historical experience. Focusing mainly on the institutional development of constitutional and legal systems, scholars explored questions of national identity and indulged in arcane discussions over the origins. The issues held certain patriotic implications. In Germany and France, medievalists such as Heinrich von Sybel and Fustel de Coulanges debated whether the primary influences shaping society had Frankish or Roman antecedents. In England, too, investigations revolved around constitutional history and the implication of the Whig interpretation, pointing to the central importance of the extension of liberty and the role of Parliament. Whether the modern English nation had its roots in ancient Anglo-Saxon or European practices became a matter of vivid significance.

Similarly, in the United States, a preoccupation with institutional history expressed national pride and a sense of national identity. In the middle of the nineteenth century, George Bancroft and other amateur, "literary" historians had rejoiced in the nation's birth and growth, seeing in the fledgling democracy indications of divine favor. Such conceptions of organic unity and supernatural direction broke down after the Civil War, in part the result of industrialization, urbanization, immigration, and class strife. As a consequence, a new generation of university-trained historians in the 1880s and 1890s sought to harness more rigorous and reliable means of historical analysis. The creation of the American Historical Association in 1884 testified to their professional commitment.

Inspired by visions of "scientific" history, American historians incorporated into their work initially the European concern for institutional growth. Early renditions traced the lineage of American liberty and democracy back to the Germanic heritage. Professor Herbert Baxter Adams preached this gospel in his famous seminar at Johns Hopkins University in Baltimore, locating the "germ" of later developments in the misty Teutonic forests. The idea, rudimentary in form, could not withstand scholarly scrutiny and dissolved under pressure from various sources, including the so-called "imperial school" of colonial history. Scholars such as Herbert L. Osgood, George Louis Beer, and Charles McLean Andrews traced the roots not to remote German villages but to the English legacies and also to the actual effects of the colonial experience in the New World.

The social dislocations of the age and the ensuing reform impetus called forth new approaches in academic scholarship, particularly in the areas of law, philosophy, social science, and history. Seeking to promote progress through reform and conscious planning, historians during the Progressive era in the United States developed what became known as the "New History." Characteristically skeptical in tone and iconoclastic in approach, the "new" historians especially regarded lofty, public statements of high-blown and idealistic purpose with suspicion, perceiving in them a subterfuge for material or selfish interests.

An early version, really a precursor, appeared in the works of Frederick Jackson Turner. In the year 1893, he read before the American Historical Association a paper on the significance of the frontier in American history. His seminal idea, "the frontier thesis," retained great influence within the historical profession for over half a century and profoundly shifted the focus of study in U. S. history. First, Turner repudiated the views of Herbert Baxter Adams, his teacher, and all notions that American institutions had germinated in the Teutonic woods. Turner saw liberty, democracy, and individualism as homegrown traits, the products of the frontier experience. Second, he shifted attention away from the eastern seaboard and New England toward the West, where in his view successive acts of settlement had engendered the laudable qualities of which he spoke. Oftentimes elusive and poetic in formulation, Turner's sparse writings never made clear whether the author understood the frontier as a place, a process, or a state of mind. Nevertheless, the Turner thesis captivated many historians because, in a single stroke, it accounted for American uniqueness and put ordinary white people, the settlers, at the center of things. It had less to offer native peoples and other victims of westward expansion.

Another among the "new" historians who shaped the consciousness of his times, Charles Austin Beard developed an economic interpretation of U. S. history. More indebted intellectually to James Madison and *The Federalist Papers* than to Karl Marx, Beard, a committed activist and reformer, first directed his attention toward the founding fathers. In 1913, the publication of *An Economic Interpretation of the Constitution* set forth daring heretical views. Emphasizing the impact of class conflicts, Beard disparaged the supposed effects of altruistic impulses and providential designs by underscoring the complex interplay of material concerns. Indeed, he characterized the clash as a contest between a popular party based on paper money and agrarian preoccupations and a conservative party founded upon urban, financial, mercantile, and personal property interests. For Beard, the adoption of the Constitution, a triumph for the latter, really amounted to a kind of counterrevolution against the alleged democratic excesses under the Articles of Confederation. In a later work entitled *The Rise of American Civilization*, first published in 1934, Beard and his collaborator, his wife Mary, gave special prominence to economic causes and argued the case that U. S. history consistently had pitted the selfishness of the business classes against the well-being of the people.

Especially poignant during the decade of the Great Depression, such themes figured prominently in the Progressive school of historiography in the United States. During these years of political and economic upheaval, Progressive historians retained hopes for the future and expressed a cherished regard for democratic traditions out of concern for maintaining them in a violent industrial age. Through the mechanisms of social science, rationality, cooperation, and planning, they hoped to retain the best of the past in the years to come and also sought to facilitate through their scholarship the very cause of reform.

The major works by Progressive historians centered on conflict in the American experience, defined either in class or sectional terms. In a study of the origins of the American Revolution, *A History of Political Parties in the Province of New York, 1768–1776* (1909), Carl L. Becker depicted a struggle not only against English authority but against the dominant, colonial oligarchy, possessing a monopolistic hold on power and wealth. As Becker noted, the issue became a question not only of home rule but also of who should rule at home. The sectional emphasis, to an extent inspired by Frederick Jackson Turner, gave a conspicuous role in competition among regions with distinctive geographic, economic, and social characteristics. When presented in this way, U. S. history turned into a story of incessant rivalry among the East, the South, and the West.

While Turner concentrated on the frontier regions and inspired an ongoing debate over the merits of his thesis for more than a generation, other scholars found inspiration in other localities and issues. The works of Vernon Parrington, Perry Miller, and Samuel Eliot Morison illuminated New England traditions, especially the Puritan heritage. The South, in spite of its "peculiar institution," that is, slavery, provoked sympathetic investigations of white elites by William A. Dunning and a cluster of historians around him. The Civil War figured as a central event for Progressive historians. Although Beard treated this climactic struggle in economic terms, portraying it as a second American Revolution bringing about the unchallenged dominance of the industrial classes, his revisionist successors, notably James G. Randall in *The Civil War and Reconstruction* (1937), explained the war as the consequence of inexplicable human folly, the catastrophic work of "a blundering generation." For Civil War scholars, the questions of causation and inevitability—that is, whether the fighting was avoidable or not—took on fundamental significance.

Oddly, Progressive historians displayed little interest in scrutinizing the course of race relations in the United States and left that writing to others. Consequently, some of it incorporated negative racial assumptions. Ulrich B. Phillips, for example, understood slavery as a way of coping with an "inferior" race. In contrast, notable black historians, such W. E. B. Du Bois and Carter G. Woodson, both educated at Harvard University, engaged in political and intellectual struggles during their long careers to enhance the understanding and the status of black people. Du Bois, for example, participated in founding the National Association for the Advancement of Colored People (NAACP) and *The Journal of Negro History.*

Though neglectful of the role of race in the United States, Progressive historians otherwise tried to write useful history in order to elucidate the nature of contemporary social issues. Indeed, their advocacy of political causes set some of them at odds with the standards of "scientific" history and raised questions about the attainability of the objective truth. For Carl Becker and Charles Beard, "that noble dream," in Beard's words, would always elude fulfillment. For historians such as Becker and Beard, public utility as much as accuracy should guide the construction of historical narratives. When Beard spoke dubiously of objectivity before the American Historical Association in 1935, he raised a storm over his dangerous flirtation with the doctrine of relativism. If the criterion of objectivity could not hold, then historians could never assure themselves that they knew anything at all. The issue is addressed fully in Peter Novick's book, *That Noble Dream: The "Objectivity Question" and the American Historical Association* (1988).

Doubt and uncertainty assailed historians all over the world during the decade of the Great Depression, although in some countries totalitarian renditions provided the illusion of safe haven. In Italy, fascism exalted the leadership principle and identified Benito Mussolini as the manifestation of the national will but failed to impose this version of reality upon important Italian intellectuals. Benedetto Croce, a philosopher and historian, dissented from fascist orthodoxy, and Antonio Gramsci, a Marxist sociologist, paid for his opposition with his life. Similarly, in Germany the doctrines of National Socialism and the racism attached to them created havoc within the universities and resulted in purges of Jewish professors, sacrificing some of the best minds in that country. Nazi historiography functioned as propaganda by venerating German warriors, military power, and the authority of the state. The legacies of the Nazi debacle left future generations of German historians with the obligation to wrestle with the problems of guilt and responsibility.

In the Soviet Union, meanwhile, Marxism became the state ideology. Though traditionally much influenced by German conceptions of rigor and objectivity, Russian historians of bourgeois origin became suspect during the Stalin era when, indeed, the dictator intervened in academic disputes in order to ensure "correct" interpretations. As a consequence, Bolshevik doctrines became unassailable and the Russian Revolution an unquestioned anticipation of the future. According to the orthodox view, the Soviet Union would assume leadership in bringing about the fulfillment of Marxist-Leninist prophecies and the establishment of world communism. For a time during the Second World War, termed "the Great Patriotic War" in Russian, the desperation of the life-and-death struggle called forth an emphasis on more traditional nationalism. Subsequently, the reappearance of the hard-line Stalinist version after the peace reaffirmed the hegemony of the official ideology not only within the Soviet Union but over "the peoples' republics" in Eastern Europe as well.

Elsewhere in the world, Marxian scholars, removed from Stalin's authority, struggled with the intellectual puzzles of reconciling fact with theory and thought with practice. Among the members of the so-called "Frankfurt school" in Germany during the 1930s, critical thinkers repudiated simple-minded varieties of "vulgar" Marxism, featuring an undue economic emphasis, and urged a fuller appreciation of the diversity of influences shaping human behavior. Erich Fromm, for example, sought some form of amalgamation with psychoanalysis. During the Hitler years, the dispersion of the Frankfurt school into other countries introduced the constituents (for example, Herbert Marcuse) to the rigors of Anglo-Saxon empiricism and at the same time invigorated more conventional thinking outside Germany with exposure to sophisticated Marxian analysis.

French scholars also participated in the effort to obtain more comprehensive forms of understanding of the human past. Led by

Marc Bloch and Lucien Febvre, the founders in 1929 of the influential journal, *Annales d'histoire économique et sociale*, the historians making up the "*Annales* school" rebelled against the prevailing forms of academic history. Rejecting the narrow emphasis on politics, war, and diplomacy, what Febvre disparaged as *histoire événementielle*, that is, event-oriented history, the *Annales* group strove to grasp more totally and fully the many dimensions of human reality. As the historiographer Ernst Breisach explained, these French scholars envisioned a new, more complete history, inclusive of all aspects of human life. To achieve the aim, they aspired to the development of a larger repertoire of investigatory techniques and called for extensive cooperation with "comrades and brothers" across the entire span of social and human sciences. As Febvre expressed the goal, "Down with all barriers and labels! At the frontiers, astride the frontiers, with one foot on each side, that is where the historian has to work, freely, usefully."[2]

The tenets of the *Annales* group triumphed among French historians after 1945, testifying in part to a sense of disenchantment with the practice and values of the old France, a principal loser in the Second World War. Resuming publication under a new title, *Annales: Economies, societés, civilisation*, *Annaliste* scholars resumed their quest for more total history. Surprisingly, although their work had implications for historical theory and methodology, they wrote little on such subjects. During the war, famed medievalist Marc Bloch, a hunted resistance fighter later executed by the Nazis, composed a book, *The Historian's Craft*, a modest methodological survey but hardly a manifesto. By and large, *Annales* scholars left their theoretical and methodological assumptions implicitly in their other writings.

Two traits figured conspicuously. First, *Annaliste* scholars typically built their analyses around a conception of collective consciousness. Termed *mentalité*, this phenomenon focused attention on the mental and psychological characteristics of groups of people at specified times and places and thus moved historians beyond constrictive and sometimes myopic concerns with mere individuals. According to this approach, the collectivity counted most in the formulation of explanations leading to total history. Second, in similar fashion, *Annaliste* historians employed a notion of the *longue durée*, the long duration. Actually a conception of time, this term depicted the structural continuities intruding upon the course of historical change. The *longue durée*, among other things, comprised the land, the sea, the climate, and the vegetation. These conditions affirmed stabilizing influences over the conduct of human affairs and impelled a slower pace or rhythm than the transitory events of politics, war, and diplomacy. They determined, moreover, the manner of life.

The best-known work by an *Annaliste* historian, Fernand Braudel's *The Mediterranean World in the Age of Philip II* first appeared in 1949 with a second edition in 1966. It set forth ambitious aims, seeking to encompass the whole, that is, the totality of life in the region, focusing upon the uniformities in the political, social, economic, intellectual, and geographic realms. Braudel's concern for the continuities of life, the overarching structures of time, and the languid pace of change, and also his efforts to develop conceptual unities, obtained many impressive results but, according to his critics, seldom achieved the desired level of integration. The sheer magnitude of the task militated against the fulfillment of his good intentions but nevertheless inspired successors in the *Annales* school, such as Emmanuel Le Roy Ladurie, who wrote on peasants and rural civilization; Philippe Ariès, who studied childhood and death; and W. H. T. Beezley, who dealt with Mexican folkways in the late nineteenth century. Beezley's book, *Judas at the Jockey Club and Other Episodes of Porfirian Mexico* (1987), described the transformation of a traditional custom into a form of contemporary political protest when dissenters made Judas Iscariot dolls to look like hated local leaders and then either burned or blew them up. Such innovative works kept alive the ideal of total history.

In the United States, the impact of the Second World War and its aftermath shook the foundations of Progressive historiography. Indeed, successive cataclysmic horrors instilled new appreciations for indeterminacy and uncertainty, some things of which the Europeans had a firmer grasp. Simple verities lost appeal. As Reinhold Niebuhr explained in *The Irony of American History* (1952), even the best of intentions could go awry, resulting in error and terrible excess. The Progressive school's commitment to plain dualities, the juxtaposition of selfish business interests against the democratic will of the people, held less credibility, and as a consequence new ornate and more problematic conceptions of historical realities came to the fore.

The publication in 1945 of Arthur M. Schlesinger's important work, *The Age of Jackson*, constituted a kind of monument to the attainments of Progressive historiography. Though subtly put, it developed a characteristic argument favoring the continuity of reform as the savior of American politics from Thomas Jefferson to Andrew Jackson to Franklin Roosevelt, but with an intriguing twist. Rather than find the impetus to reform among agrarians and westerners (the Turner view), Schlesinger located it among urban workers and eastern liberals. Schlesinger's book set off a flurry of research, writing, and reevaluation. Although some scholars still operated within the context of the Progressive tradition, notably Merrill Jensen in his study of the United States during the Articles of Confederation, *The New Nation* (1950), and Eric F. Goldman's work on reform movements since 1870, *Rendezvous with Destiny* (1952), the dominant historiographic tendency in the immediate future put a quite different construction upon the American past.

Richard Hofstadter's *The American Political Tradition and the Men Who Made It* (1948) heralded the shift. Widely read and immensely influential, it lamented the current "lack of confidence in the American future" and "the rudderless state of American liberalism." Fearful that the experiences of history had not prepared the American people to respond creatively in the years to come, Hofstadter found the fault in a traditionally opportunistic style of political leadership, "a democracy of cupidity," and an absence of truly fundamental differences separating liberals from conservatives. Because the two groups habitually agreed upon essentials, for example, the legitimacy of profit incentives and private property, the Progressive emphasis upon conflict in U. S. history obscured the basic reality. Quite the contrary, according to Hofstadter, the main contenders for power affirmed a consensus in support of the business and capitalism.

Hofstadter sounded the theme so characteristic of historical thinking in the 1950s, and other scholars soon elaborated on it from different points of view. Perhaps part of a collective effort to obtain stable moorings in a sea of global change, scholars agreed that homogeneity more than disparity marked the American experience and that consensus held more explanatory power than conflict. But they differed over the reasons. In *The Liberal Tradition in America* (1955), Louis Hartz, a political scientist, explained the uniformities by arguing that Lockean assumptions about political reality bound together the American people. Born directly into the modern world, unlike the Europeans, they had no feudal structures and titled nobility from which true conservatism could emerge. In *The Americans: The Colonial*

*Experience* (1958), Daniel Boorstin attributed the cause to the stark, ineluctable, and practical necessities of surviving in the New World, and David M. Potter, in *People of Plenty: Economic Abundance and the American Character* (1954), found it rooted in material conditions.

Historians in postwar America also reacted against the relativistic implications of Progressive historiography and sought to develop more reliable methodologies capable of producing verifiable results. Characteristically, these scholars looked toward the social sciences and quantification techniques. In an important work entitled *The Concept of Jacksonian Democracy* (1961), Lee Benson employed statistical analysis in order to show that Arthur Schlesinger's categories in *The Age of Jackson* would not hold up in New York state and hence that the description of the party and class alignments lacked veracity. Though the prospect of obtaining precise measurements in such matters has held allure ever since the ancient Greeks, the drive to use numbers turned into a kind of crusade and gained momentum, in spite of Schlesinger's put-down. As Schlesinger phrased it, "As a humanist, I am bound to reply...that almost all important questions are important precisely because they are not susceptible to quantitative answers."[3]

Unsurprisingly, quantification and the use of social scientific methodology first took hold in economic history. As a discipline, economics yielded early to systemic analysis and econometrics, both of which viewed reality as consisting of coherent systems, the parts of which combined in linkages one with the other according to strict patterns. In any such arrangement, changes in any one part necessarily resulted in transformations of the whole. Moreover, mathematical models theoretically could provide the means to analyze, to assess, and to predict the consequences and the magnitudes of change, thereby, in effect, obtaining the standards of the natural sciences.

In the United States after 1945, the "New Economic history," or "cliometrics," aimed at achieving such methodological sophistication. No longer would economic historians describe and explain specific kinds of events. Instead, they would attain greater universality by scrutinizing categories of events, aggregates, and group behavior. Among the foremost practitioners, Robert W. Fogel, in a book entitled *Railroads and American Economic Growth: Essays in Econometric History* (1964), affirmed a controversial claim. Seeking to test the thesis that railroads held central importance in the economic development of the United

States, Fogel developed carefully framed models to control variables and to explore a counterfactual hypothesis. Would the absence of railroads have made any difference? Remarkably, he concluded, no, it would not, because Americans would have found alternative kinds of transportation. In a second book, *Time on the Cross: The Economics of American Negro Slavery* (1974), Fogel and colleague Stanley L. Engerman stirred up a profound dispute by depicting "the peculiar institution," contrary to prevailing views, as efficient, profitable, and conducive to a standard of living, defined exclusively in material terms, at least as high as that of Northern workers. Critics responded with denunciations of this work as a methodological monstrosity, reminiscent of antiabolitionist propaganda before the Civil War.

If quantification could obtain such levels of meaning in economic history, why not also in other areas? To an extent following the lead of the *Annales* school in France, various historians proposed to employ such means in the pursuit of more total forms of understanding. Statistical analysis and counting became the orders of the day in the "new" political and social histories, and the tasks of collecting, storing, and processing the data became ever easier because of modern computers. Accordingly, the utilization of collective biographies within influential groups and the exhaustive examination of election returns affirmed demonstrable conclusions about political behavior. Presumably, the same held true in investigations centering on the formation of elites, the distribution of property ownership, the degree of social mobility, and the demographic structure. In the latter case, amazingly, through the proper use of projections and approximations based on population statistics and parish records, historians could arrive at reasonably exact rates of marriage, fertility, and mortality. Often unimpressed by such attainments, more traditional historians sometimes regarded them as mere shows of manipulative virtuosity, dazzling performances in which the means of investigation too frequently turned into ends in themselves. The critics wondered whether an understanding of history really benefited much. In response, William O. Aydelotte defended quantification in history with the modest claim that it provided "a means of verifying general statements."[4]

Another proposed use of social science advised the application of psychoanalytical theory. Though less precise than mathematical formulations, this endeavor also strove for deeper forms of understanding. Focusing on individual behavior, it normally found the wellspring of action in the human psyche, particularly in the conflict between inner drives and outer constraints. For orthodox Freudians, the experiences of infancy and the relations with parents and siblings held special importance in shaping the future adult. For example, the much-lamented and unfortunate psychoanalytical biography of Woodrow Wilson by William C. Bullitt and Sigmund Freud, *Thomas Woodrow Wilson: A Psychological Study* (1967), attributed the man's deficiencies, notably his need to fail, to the incapacities of the boy and his inability to satisfy the demands of an insatiable father.

Psychohistory, the amalgamation of psychoanalytical theory with history, acquired growing influence in the United States after 1945, in part because of diminished faith in reason and progress and also because of an influx of European experts. Their views won over influential American historians, for example William Langer of Harvard University, and encouraged the utilization of Freud's findings in order to plumb the depths of the psyche. According to psychohistorians, a greater awareness of the role of unreason in human behavior would result in better history.

The ensuing scholarly efforts have had mixed results. Because effective psychohistory compels expertise in two demanding disciplines, the requirements sometimes have exceeded the capabilities of individual practitioners and have produced inadvertently comic consequences. In more capable hands, in contrast, psychoanalytical techniques employing theories of character formation have achieved notable results. Examples would include Erik H. Erikson, *Young Man Luther* (1958), David H. Donald, *Charles Sumner and the Coming of the Civil War* (1960), and Fawn M. Brodie, *Richard Nixon: The Shaping of His Character* (1981). Yet even such expert works raised compelling questions, persuading dubious observers to resist some of the inflated claims of champions, such as Lloyd de Mause, who saw in psychohistory an emerging science of human motivation. Critics mounted attacks from two main directions. On the one hand, they assailed the tendency to reduce history to individual biography, thereby endorsing new versions of the old-fashioned and discredited Great Man (or Human) theory. On the other, they skeptically appraised the possibility of verifying any claims set forth. Indeed, according to this view, psychohistory entailed the most blatant of empathetic leaps into the heads of historical actors and allowed for no believable methods of

proof at all. Groundless and theoretical, it set forth no means of verification. The body of critical works include Jacques Barzun's *Clio and
the Doctors: PsychoHistory, Quanto-History & History* (1974) and David
E. Stannard's *Shrinking History: On Freud and the Failure of Psychohistory* (1980). In contrast, Peter Gay's *Freud for Historians* (1985) argues
the case in favor of psychohistory. Gay has formal training in each
area, employs psychohistorical techniques in his publications, and
wrote one of the best biographies of Freud.

Though the precepts of social-scientific history remained a
source of inspiration for many historians, others in the 1960s and
after harkened back in a sense to the traditions of Progressive historiography. Seeking to put political commitments back into their narratives, they preferred contemporary relevance over scientific
detachment and sought, much as the Progressives had, to elucidate
current issues through historical inquiries. The conduct of foreign affairs, race relations, gender issues, and the use and abuse of political
and economic power became objects of compelling concern. Obviously reflecting current cares over the Vietnam War, the civil rights
movement, the drive for women's liberation, gay and lesbian rights,
and the Watergate affair, many historians making up the so-called
"New Left" reworked the usual versions of U. S. history. Characteristically, they sought more radical perspectives, for example, by incorporating viewpoints from "the underside"—that is, outlooks
representative of class, racial, ethnic, and gender groups previously
rendered invisible in many traditional historical accounts. Often
harshly critical in tone, New Left historiography usually depicted
the established system as rapacious, exploitative, and racist in character, and often attributed such excesses in some measure to the conditions of economic capitalism. Though aspiring to avoid dogmatism,
most New Left historians maintained that Marxism had applicabili-
ty to the American experience.

Such revisionism challenged more orthodox historiography on
many points and raised firestorms of dispute. An early statement,
William Appleman Williams's *The Tragedy of American Diplomacy*
(1959) repudiated the usual interpretation emphasizing the good if oftentimes futile intentions of the United States by depicting the country's foreign policy as the product of capitalist proclivities. According
to Williams, the Marxian emphasis on markets, trade, and profits
held true. Consequently, a group of his students and associates at the

University of Wisconsin elaborated upon such themes, constituting the so-called "Wisconsin school." Walter LaFeber's *The New Empire: An Interpretation of American Expansion, 1860–1898* (1963), for example, set forth an economic interpretation of U. S. expansion during the late nineteenth century, and Lloyd C. Gardner's *Architects of Illusion: Men and Ideas in American Foreign Policy, 1941–1949* (1970) did the same for the early Cold War era. In 1993, LaFeber published *The American Search for Opportunity, 1865–1913*, volume 2 in *The Cambridge History of American Foreign Relations*, thirty years later covering the same period as the earlier work and arguing even more emphatically in favor of an economic interpretation. This work also underscored the destabilizing and revolutionary effects of United States capitalism when projected into other, less-developed countries. Indeed, infusions of capitalist enterprise proved to be the most potent, revolutionary impetus during the era.

Such New Left renditions and other efforts inspired by social, cultural, and political change impelled searching reevaluations of United States history and veered off in many directions. Some historians depicted the economic system as a corporate entity, designed, controlled, and maintained by ruling elites with immense exploitative capabilities. Others explored relationships based on class, race, and gender. Such studies illuminated the experiences of laboring people, ethnic and racial groups, women, children, and families. The tide of publications in the area of gender studies also included significant works on lesbians and gays. Such outcomes, surely provocative and challenging, showed the feasibility of doing history while incorporating attitudes and viewpoints other than those associated with white male elites; they also promoted a degree of conceptual fragmentation.

The more traditional narratives, focusing on the activities of white male elites, had presumed commonalities of experience and supposed that such stories spoke for everyone. The newer histories, in contrast, raised questions and insisted upon distinctions. For example, when the civil rights movement in the 1950s and 1960s riveted public attention on race relations in the United States, the initial historical works by and large dealt with the issue as it seemed to whites. This approach never satisfied the aggrieved minorities. The black perspective later emerged in important works such as John W. Blassingame's *The Slave Community: Plantation Life in the*

*Antebellum South* (1972) and Eugene D. Genovese's *Roll, Jordan, Roll: The World the Slaves Made* (1974). These books tried to comprehend the institution of slavery from the inside, that is, by showing how it appeared to and affected black people and how they coped with the circumstances.

Similarly, the writing of women's history posed profound conceptual problems. Women in the feminist movement properly complained that textbook history particularly had rendered them invisible through exclusion. They just did not show up. Although to be sure a few historians had written about women, the publications consisted of a particular sort, focusing either on great women, such as Joan of Arc or Queen Elizabeth I, or political activists in the reform and suffrage movements, such as Jane Addams. Critics observed correctly that women had to act like men in order to merit attention.

The new scholarship often conveyed a feminist emphasis and insisted upon putting ordinary women into the historical narratives. Neither "great" nor necessarily politically active, they included middle-class women, immigrants, ethnics, and all racial groups. Yet, the mere organization of the material presented puzzles for the obvious reason. Traditional historians had derived the very categories in which they thought from the world of males. For example, chronological schemes based on kingly reigns or presidential administrations, economic cycles, or warfare had nothing intrinsically to do with women. The format of the conventional textbook, in short, had scant relevance. How then to incorporate the history of women?

This question pressed heavily upon scholars and allowed for no single solution. In a groundbreaking book entitled *Woman's Proper Place: A History of Changing Ideals and Practices, 1870 to the Present* (1978), Sheila Rothman suggested one response. For her, the study of women in history required an approach consisting of three parts. First, historians must comprehend the roles and responsibilities assigned to women in any given period. Next, the scholars must determine the degree to which various women of different classes and races actually adhered to those demarcations. Last, they must carefully observe the process of change, the shifting definitions of women's proper place over time, and the degrees to which the various categories of women actually complied with them. Books such as *Liberty's Daughters: The Revolutionary Experience of American Woman, 1750-1800* (1980) and

*Founding Mothers and Fathers: Gendered Power and the Forming of American Society* (1996) by Mary Beth North and *The Girl Problem: Female Sexual Delinquency in New York, 1900-1930* (1995) by Ruth M. Alexander establish models for such forms of historical writing.

In recent times, various conceptual and methodological conundrums have confounded practitioners throughout the discipline of history and to an extent have erected barriers against communication. Highly specialized in their expertise, historians sometimes lament that they have difficulty understanding and appreciating the work of colleagues in other fields. In the 1980s and 1990s, some with traditionalistic inclinations also proclaimed that such conditions had produced a crisis within the discipline. Warning against some of the implications of the present-day emphasis on "diversity" and "multiculturalism," Arthur M. Schlesinger, Jr., has advised against ever allowing history to degenerate into a form of therapy designed to promote personal self-esteem. Similarly, Theodore S. Hamerow has expressed his fear that history as a discipline has lost its traditional intellectual standing as a unifier of knowledge, and Gertrude Himmelfarb has cautioned against misunderstanding, misconception, and other bad effects when historians shift attention excessively to disadvantaged groups and away from the politically powerful who define established systems. Recently, Joyce Appleby, Lynn Hunt, and Margaret Jacob in a judicious, thoughtful book, *Telling the Truth about History*, in many ways a defense of new kinds of social and cultural history, warn nevertheless about some of the implications of recent developments in critical literary theory for history. Called postmodernism, this body of thinking questions such fundamentals as reason, objectivity, and the knowability of the past, suggesting thereby that historical narratives differ hardly at all from fiction.

In reaction against intellectual fragmentation and uncertainty, Thomas Bender, among others, has advised in favor of creating a new synthesis in United States history around a conception of what he called "public culture," that is, an attempt to amalgamate the new history with the old. Whether such appeals will have much effect remains an issue for the future as historians grapple with the problem. At present, the cacophony of voices produced by clashing stratagems and rival interests seems to allow for no immediate resolution. Indeed, it represents to an extent a profound demographic change affecting the scholars in the profession. No longer dominated by the well-to-do scions of aristocratic, east-coast families, the practitioners of history as a professional discipline include many historians who made their way into the universities after the Second World War because of the G.I. Bill, the National Defense Education Act, and other such public programs. Happily, they comprised within their ranks persons of various and oftentimes modest origins whose objects of study testified to their diversity. Together, employing many different angles of vision, they now participate in the collective enterprise of writing history.

Although particularities and divergences of many sorts characterize the craft of history in the present day, one thing seems reasonably clear. History no longer sets forth common stories that presumably speak for the identity and experience of all readers. For many consumers of history, the narratives centering on the activities of white male elites no longer provide either satisfaction, stimulation, or a means to truth. We no longer possess a past commonly agreed upon. Indeed, to the contrary, we have a multiplicity of versions competing for attention and emphasizing alternatively elites or nonelites, men or women, whites or persons of color, and no good way of reconciling all the differences. Though the disparities and the incoherences create terrible predicaments for historians who prize orderliness in their stories, such conditions also aptly express the confusions of the world and the experiences of different people in it. If historians can agree on little else, at least they should rejoice in the realization that they have many true stories to tell about the human past.

## RECOMMENDED READINGS

The following titles, highly selective, represent a large body of scholarship. *Historians at Work*, volumes 3 and 4, *Niebuhr to Maitland*, and *Dilthy to Hofstadter* (New York: Harper and Row, 1975), by Peter Gay, Victor G. Wexler, and Gerald J. Cavanaugh, show the shift from the nineteenth to the twentieth century. *Historiography: Ancient, Medieval & Modern*, 2nd ed. (Chicago, IL: University of Chicago Press, 1994), by Ernst Breisach, spells out the details and contains a splendid bibliography. Other books delineate trends and current tendencies, among them, *The Past Before Us: Contemporary Historical Writing in the United States* (Ithaca, NY: Cornell University Press, 1980), ed. Michael Kammen; *Historical Studies Today* (New York: W. W. Norton, 1972), ed. Felix Gilbert and Stephen R. Graubard; and *History: The Development of Historical Studies in the United States* (Englewood Cliffs, NJ: Prentice-Hall, 1965), by John Higham, Leonard Krieger, and Felix Gilbert. Marc Bloch's classic discussion of methodology is contained in *The Historian's Craft*, trans. Peter Putnam (New York: Vintage Books, 1953).

Works on specific historians include Richard Hofstadter, *The Progressive Historians: Turner, Beard, Parrington* (New York: Alfred A. Knopf, 1969); Lee Benson, *Turner and Beard: American Historical Writing Reconsidered* (New York: The Free Press, 1960); Harvey Wish, ed., *American Historians: A Selection* (New York: Oxford University Press, 1962); and Earl E. Thorpe, *Black Historians: A Critique* (New York: William Morrow, 1971). John Barker, *The Super-Historians: Makers of Our Past* (New York: Charles Scribner's Sons, 1982), contains an essay on W. E. B. Du Bois. The views of Charles A. Beard and Carl Becker are set forth in "That Noble Dream," *American Historical Review*, 41 (Oct. 1935); and *Everyman His Own Historian: Essays on History and Politics* (New York: F. S. Crofts, 1935). Other works include Ray Allen Billington, *Frederick Jackson Turner: Historian, Scholar, Teacher* (New York: Oxford University Press, 1973); Carole Fink, *Marc Bloch: A Life in History* (Cambridge: Cambridge University Press, 1989); John Kenyon, *The History Men: The Historical Profession in England since the Renaissance* (University of Pittsburgh Press, 1984), and Peter Burke, *The French Historical Revolution: The Annales School, 1929–1989* (Palo Alto, CA: Stanford University Press, 1990).

Insights into the ongoing debates over research methods are obtained in *Historical Analysis: Contemporary Approaches to Clio's Craft* (New York: John Wiley, 1978), ed. Richard E. Beringer; *Toward the Scientific Study of History: Selected Essays* (New York: J. B. Lippincott Company, 1972), by Lee Benson; *American Historical Explanations: A Strategy for Grounded Inquiry* (Homewood, IL: Dorsey Press, 1973), by Gene Wise; *A Behavioral Approach to Historical Analysis of Historical Data* (Homewood, IL: Dorsey Press, 1969), ed. D. K. Rowney and J. Q. Graham; *Quantification in History* (Reading, MA: Addison-Wesley, 1971), by William O. Aydelotte; and *Which Road to the Past? Two Views of History* (New Haven, CT: Yale University Press, 1983), by G. R. Elton and Robert W. Fogel. Jacques Barzun, *Clio and the Doctors: PsychoHistory, Quanto-History & History* (Chicago, IL: University of Chicago Press, 1974), and David E. Stannard, *Shrinking History: On Freud and the Failure of Psychohistory* (New York: Oxford University Press, 1980), raise probing questions. Peter Gay, *Freud for Historians* (New York: Oxford University Press, 1985), defends the viability of psychohistory. Ronald Takaki, *A Different Mirror: A History of Multicultural America* (Boston: Little, Brown, 1993), tells the story from the viewpoint of diverse persons of color. On the contemporary "crisis" in history, commentary appears in Theodore S. Hamerow, *Reflections on History and Historians* (Madison: University of Wisconsin Press, 1987); Gertrude Himmelfarb, *The New*

*History and the Old* (Cambridge, MA: The Belknap Press of Harvard University Press, 1987); and Thomas Bender, "Wholes and Parts: The Need for Synthesis in American History," *The Journal of American History, 73* (June 1986). Arthur M. Schlesinger, Jr., *The Disuniting of America* (W. W. Norton, 1992) warns of impending danger when history is looked upon as a kind of therapy to build personal self-esteem. Finally, *Telling the Truth about History* (New York: W. W. Norton, 1994), by Joyce Appleby, Lynn Hunt, and Margaret Jacob, explores the emergence of history as an academic discipline in modern times and addresses many important epistemological issues, including postmodernism. The same is true of Georg G. Iggers, *Historiography in the Twentieth Century: From Scientific Objectivity to the Postmodern Challenge* (Hanover, NH: University Press of New England, 1997.

Articles on historiography sometimes appear in *The American Historical Review*. Recent issues contain "Annaliste Paradigm? The Geohistorical Structure of Fernand Braudel," *86* (February 1981), by Samuel Kinser; "The Contribution of Women to Modern Historiography in Great Britain, France, and the United States, 1750-1940," *89* (June 1984), by Bonnie Smith; and "Guilt, Redemption, and Writing German History," *88* (February 1983), by Theodore S. Hamerow. The volume devoted to *The American Historical Association: The First Hundred Years, 1884–1984, 89* (October 1984), features essays on "Historical Consciousness in Nineteenth-Century America," by Dorothy Ross; "Beyond Consensus: Richard Hofstadter and American Historiography," by Daniel Joseph Singal; and "J. Franklin Jameson, Carter G. Woodson, and the Foundations of Black Historiography," by August Meier and Elliott Rudwick.

## ENDNOTES

1. Quoted in Ernest Breisach, *Historiography: Ancience, Medieval, and Modern,* 2nd ed. (Chicago, IL: University of Chicago Press, 1994), 285.
2. Breisach, *Historiography,* 370–371.
3. Quoted in Breisach, *Historiography,* 341.
4. Quoted in Breisach, *Historiography,* 340.

# Postscript:

## *Culture Wars and Postmodernism*

During the 1990s, professional history of the sort favored by most academic historians became embroiled in a sequence of notable controversies. Some of them, carried out in the public arena, placed history at the center of rampaging culture wars in the United States. Such encounters usually came about when militant, outspoken, and influential groups that possessed fixed and traditional views about history attacked so-called "revisionists" supposedly for misrepresenting, demeaning, and subverting their preferred and more orthodox accounts of the past. One especially heated altercation developed over a proposed display at the Smithsonian Institution in Washington, D. C., intended in 1995 to mark the fiftieth anniversary of the atomic bombing of Hiroshima at the end of the Second World War.

Another form of contention, more theoretical in nature, caused other kinds of acrimony among scholars at professional meetings and in learned journals. The source of the difficulty in this instance, a body of thinking known as postmodernism, unsettled historians by challenging the precepts upon which they based their work. Indeed, by repudiating Enlightenment conceptions of reason, objectivity, and progress and emphasizing the self-contained nature of all language, postmodern theorists allow for no distinction between history and fiction, seeking thereby to collapse the former into the latter. To maintain the integrity of their discipline, historians as a consequence have a need, on the one hand, to instruct historical fundamentalists who insist upon sacred and sancrosanct versions of an unchanging past and, on the other, to persuade unbelieving skeptics who deny its knowability.

The Smithsonian Institution moved into the center of the culture wars early in the 1990s by developing plans to put on display an exhibition featuring the fuselage of the *Enola Gay*, the B-29 Superfortress that dropped the atomic bomb on Hiroshima on 6 August 1945. The proposed exhibition, in the works for some time, had obtained the support of Martin Harwit, the new museum director, formerly an astrophysicist from Cornell University, and a naturalized U.S. citizen from Czechoslovakia whose family had fled from the Nazis. Harwit had vivid memories of the Second World War and wanted the Smithsonian Institution to take up important questions "that are under public debate." [1] The proposed *Enola Gay* display held promise for this purpose but also entailed certain risks. What kind of an exhibit on atomic warfare could possibly satisfy all viewers?

As historian Peter Novick told an audience on National Public Radio in January 1995, "There are all sorts of different, alternative, and legitimate ways of framing the story of Hiroshima." In elaboration, he explained:

> You can frame it as the veterans appear to want, as the culmination of America's response to unprovoked Japanese aggression. You can frame it as a chapter in the history of white atrocities against nonwhites, as an episode in the escalating barbarization of warfare in the twentieth century. You could talk about it as the opening of the terrifying age of potential nuclear devastation.

In other words, Novick argued, there is no one "truth" about Hiroshima. Historical accounts are always "radically selective narrativizations of events."[2]

The museum curators wrote a script of more than 300 pages to go along with the display. They sought accuracy, balance, thoroughness, and connectedness with modern scholarship. For example, the opening section criticized the Japanese for pursuing a kind of expansionism "marked by naked aggression and extreme brutality." It also established significant distinctions. For most Americans, according to the proposed narrative, the Pacific war differed from the European conflict in important respects. Because of racism and Pearl Harbor, the fighting against Japan turned into "a war of vengeance."

For the Japanese in contrast, "it was a war to defend their unique culture against Western imperialism." Such claims impressed critics as unacceptable; for them, they were too hard on the United States and too easy on Japan.[3]

The other four parts of the script also gave offense. In the second section entitled "The Decision to Drop the Bomb," the text set forth an accurate but debatable proposition by arguing that "alternatives for ending the Pacific War other than an invasion or atomic-bombing were available, but are more obvious in hindsight than they were at the time." Other uncertainties also appeared as unresolved questions. Would the United States have employed the bomb against Germany? Did U.S. leaders unwisely ignore Japanese peace feelers? To what extent, if at all, was the bomb intended to influence Soviet behavior in Europe? Quotations from General Dwight D. Eisenhower and other wartime leaders expressed misgivings about the necessity of using the atomic bomb.

In the third and fourth sections, more reasons for controversy appeared in discussions of the means of "Delivering the Bomb" and the effects at "Ground Zero." The text emphasized the role of Colonel Paul Tibbets, the pilot of the *Enola Gay* who led the mission, as well as the military significance of the B-29 Superfortress in the air campaigns against Japan and the consequences of the atomic bombing for the people of Hiroshima. The Smithsonian's plans called for the use of various artifacts to illustrate the human effects and the horror. Finally in the last section, "The Legacy of Hiroshima and Nagasaki," the proposed commentary reviewed the events leading to Japan's surrender, the obduracy of Japanese military hardliners who resisted capitulation in spite of Hiroshima and Nagasaki, and the subsequent collapse of the wartime alliance with the Soviet Union, leading to the onset of the Cold War. The conclusion pointed to ongoing dilemmas and paradoxes during the atomic age, highlighting the obvious. Now that the nuclear genie had gotten out of the bottle, no good way existed to put it back in again.

As the narrative took shape early in 1993, leaders at the Smithsonian Institution tried to keep interested observers informed of the contents and to avoid the obvious pitfalls of bias, misrepresentation, and error. A nine-member advisory committee consisting of historians and one combat veteran of the Pacific war provided a critique, cautioning against too celebratory a tone in favor of the United States.

Veterans' groups had different reactions. The powerful Air Force Association, a lobby, especially reacted with disfavor and became the leader in the ensuing fight. According to John T. Correll, the executive director of the AFA, the Smithsonian Institution had erred egregiously by treating Japan and the United States "as if their participation in the war were morally equivalent." According to Correll, "Japanese aggression and atrocities seem to have no significant place in this account."[4]

As viewed by the Air Force Association and other such organizations, the proposed exhibition failed fundamentally to commemorate properly the heroism, suffering, and self-sacrifice of U.S. soldiers and sailors during the Pacific war and by so doing displayed insufficient appreciation. It also showed too much sympathy for the Japanese and defied the conviction of many veterans who believed that President Truman's use of the bomb had saved their lives by making a costly invasion of Japan unnecessary. As a consequence, according to Hubert R. Dagley II, an official of the American Legion, many veterans believed that museum curators and academic historians had defamed them by treating their experiences condescendingly, if indeed not contemptuously. Accordingly, they had scant patience with historical accounts pointing to the vindictiveness of the U.S. war effort or to Truman's alleged efforts to gain leverage over the Soviets through atomic diplomacy. Who, after all, started the war in the first place?

In response, the Smithsonian Institution authorized a variety of changes, modifications, and clarifications in the text but failed to satisfy the critics. According to Edward T. Linenthal, one of the historians engaged with the controversy, the museum managers faced attacks on many fronts—"from journalists and media commentators, from Congress, from outraged veterans and citizens angered by news accounts." Indeed, the narrative became "an embattled text, attacked, defended, and endlessly revised in an increasingly embittered atmosphere that revealed more about American cultural politics in the 1990s than about the mission of the *Enola Gay* and the decision to drop the bomb." As Linenthal explains, "What emerged was not only a vitriolic conflict over a museum exhibition but a public relations disaster for the Smithsonian and a real threat to its budget, most of which came from congressionally appropriated funds."

The critics assailed the curators and historians for indulging in "revisionist" and "politically correct" versions of the past and supposedly for rewriting history in ways that altered the true story of the Pacific war. What such criticism usually missed was the context, that is, an awareness that a debate over the use of the bomb had gone on ever since August 1945, that scholars such as Gar Alperovitz and Barton Bernstein had written extensively about it for twenty-five years, and that the experiences of American servicemen, whatever the magnitude of their heroism, bestowed upon them no special insight into the reasons for high-level decision making in the Truman administration. In this instance, personal memory and conviction clashed with the standards and techniques of professional historians, and the former won.

In November 1994, forty historians signed a letter of protest against what they characterized as the "historical cleansing" of the Hiroshima script. For them, it was "unconscionable" that "pressures from outside the museum" should prevent the presentation of "a balanced range of the historical scholarhip on the issue." But the letter had no effect. On 30 January 1995, the museum canceled the controversial exhibit and replaced it with a smaller display, featuring part of the airplane and an abbreviated text. Later in May 1995, Martin Harwit resigned his position as director of the museum, explaining that nothing less would satisfy the critics of the Smithsonian Institution.

In the end, as Linenthal observes, "everyone believed that memory and history had been abused, and the controversy over the *Enola Gay* became a useful symbol for all sides in the history wars going on in America." For the critics, the outcome represented a victory over subversives and seditionists, that is, politically correct proponents of historical revision who depict the United States as arrogant, oppressive, and racist. For historians and museum curators in contrast, the episode warned of partisan dangers and possibilities of censorship. They lamented a lost opportunity. Just possibly visitors at the Smithsonian Institution could have faced up to the complex history embodied by the *Enola Gay*.[5]

Postmodernist theorists also have challenged the way in which historians do their work. If, as the theory holds, Enlightenment ideas about reason, objectivity, and possibilities of progress have no validity and if, in addition, historical accounts differ hardly at all from fiction, then historians face an unwelcome prospect of losing the truth-affirming part of their discipline. Without appropriate techniques of verification and authentication and, indeed, without a knowable past to write about, history could not stand as a legitimate body of knowledge.

Good historians have always known that their narratives partake of literary techniques. Telling a coherent story based on evidence requires the exercise of imaginative faculties also demanded of fiction writers. At the same time, historians usually have assumed that their reliance on documents and other artifacts, that is, primary sources, have set them apart by providing a link with an actual, knowable past. To be sure, it no longer exists, but it did once. Primary sources, the surviving records, are not identical with the past but provide some means for obtaining ideas about it. Historians in this respect resemble paleontologists, who try to construct historical images of life forms in the natural world through the use of fossils and imagination.

Postmodernist challenges emanate from highly skeptical forms of philosophical thought, linguistics, and literary criticism. In some large measure, they represent disenchantment with and mistrust of Western scientific and rationalistic worldviews, typically perceived by postmodernists as justifications for the use and abuse of power and authority. For postmodernist dissenters, the very idea of objectivity has become problematical. For them, no observer can ever form statements about anything without the influence of bias, prejudice, self-interest, and personal preference. For them, notions of objectivity in history became doubly objectionable, because there is no object to behold. What we call the past is a construct of pure imagination.

Such contentions have an impressive lineage in European thought. In the nineteen century, Friedrich Nietzsche, a philosopher, dismissed history as a form of knowledge on grounds that no objectively verifiable accounts could exist independently of the partialities and inclinations of the historian. In the twentieth century, Claude Lévi Strauss, an anthropologist, called into question claims that Western scientific rationality possessed any intrinsic superiority over mythical forms of thinking. Ferdinand de Saussure, a linguist, developed a complicated analysis, holding that language shapes images of reality but does not refer to it. In subsequent elaborations by Michel Foucault, Jacques Derrida, Paul de Man, Roland Barthes, and Hayden White, a conception of language emerged as a self-contained system of signs and symbols, referring to themselves but to nothing outside. According to this view, as historiographer Georg G. Iggers explains, "the historian is always the prisoner of the world within which he thinks, and his thoughts and perceptions are conditioned by the categories of the language in which he operates." No escape is possible. The "texts" with which historians work are creations of language, referring to nothing outside. This idea, crucial for postmodernists, applies to both primary and secondary sources. Such texts possess no unambiguous meaning and can be read in many ways. When applied to the study of history, postmodernist claims mean that "in the final analysis every historical work is a literary work which has to be judged by categories of literary criticism."[6]

This line of analysis has assumed prominence in literary theory in France and the United States since the 1960s. By removing the distinction between history and literature and fact and fiction, it eliminates one of the essential parts of Western thought since Aristotle. Hayden White has pointed out and lamented "the reluctance to consider historical narratives as what they most manifestly are: verbal fictions, the contents of which are more *invented* than *found* and the forms of which have more in common with their counterparts in literature than they have with those in the sciences." Similarly, Robert Berkhofer observed: "Because normal historians try to reconcile variant interpretations by *reference* to facts rather than by arguments over the nature of narratives as such, they must presume in practice that factuality possessed some sort of coercive reality." By denying factuality, "contemporary literary theory defies the very intellectual foundations of current historical practice."[7]

This radical critique of traditional historical methodology has taken on high levels of importance in theoretical discussions of history in recent times but has had much less impact on the actual writing of history. Indeed, acceptance of the premises would render the writing of history impossible. For most traditional historians, the distinction between truth and falsehood has remained fundamental. They understand that most of their writing takes on narrative form and probably would insist in response to the postmodernist challenge that it possesses a special truth-seeking purpose, intended to recapture parts of a past that really existed. As Roger Chartier established the point, "This reference to a reality pre-existing the historical text and situated outside of it, of which the text has the function of producing an intelligible account...is what constitutes history and keeps it different from fable or falsification."[8]

To be sure, conceptions of truth have become much more complex in recent times. In all likelihood, few historians in the present day would accept notions of absolute scientific objectivity or embrace as a goal the purpose of rendering the past exactly as it really was. Moreover, many would concede valid points to the postmodernist position. History devoted exclusively to the activities of white male elites of European extraction is no longer the standard. Ideological assumptions, often teleological propositions concerned with progress and modernization, have been incorporated into the discourses of historical scholarship. Excessive deference to the authority of experts has been a feature of professional conduct in history and elsewhere. Cultural assumptions and constructs do shape human behavior in countless ways, and the history of the world outside of Europe and the United States should not be told in terms of Westernization. Yet, history and fiction are not the same, and historians who abandon the distinction do so at their own risk. Was the Holocaust during the Second World War a real or an imagined event? Advocacy of the second claim probably would appeal to Holocaust deniers but would impress most historians as profoundly immoral. Moreover, to most historians, the Holocaust will appear as the most documented atrocity in world history, and therefore it compels belief. The evidence still counts for something.

## RECOMMENDED READINGS

*History Wars: The* Enola Gay *and Other Battles for the American Past* (New York: Henry Holt and Company, 1996), edited by Edward T. Linenthal and Tom Engelhardt, presents essays on the controversy at the Smithsonian Institution. A place to get started on postmodernism is Georg G. Iggers, *Historiography in the Twentieth Century: From Scientific Objectivity to the Postmodern Challenge* (Hanover, CT: Wesleyan University Press, 1997). *The Postmodern History Reader* (London: Routledge, 1997), edited by Keith Jenkins, elucidates from a favorable viewpoint the implications of postmodernist thought for history. *The Killing of History: How A Discipline Is Being Murdered by Literary Critics and Social Critics* (Paddington, Australia: Macleay, 1996) by Keith Windschuttle is a full-scale attack. Also critical is Pauline Marie Rosenau's *Post-Modernism and the Social Sciences: Insights, Inroads, and Intrusions* (Princeton, NJ: Princeton University Press, 1992). For additional commentary, see Lynn Hunt, ed.,

*The New Cultural History* (Berkeley: University of California Press, 1989); Hayden White, *Topics of Discourse: Essays in Cultural Criticism* (Baltimore: Johns Hopkins University Press, 1978); Jan Goldstein, ed., *Foucault and the Writing of History* (Oxford, England: Blackwell, 1994); and Robert F. Berkhofer, Jr., *Beyond the Great Story: History as Text and Discourse* (Cambridge, MA: The Belknap Press of Harvard University Press, 1995).

## ENDNOTES

1. Edward T. Linenthal and Tom Engelhardt, eds., *History Wars: The* Enola Gay *and Other Battles for the American Past* (New York: Henry Holt and Company, 1996), 15.
2. Linenthal and Engelhardt, eds., *History Wars*, 28.
3. Linenthal and Engelhardt, eds., *History Wars*, 29ff.
4. Linenthal and Engelhardt, eds., *History Wars*, 35.
5. Linenthal and Engelhardt, eds., *History Wars*, 39, 44, 52, 58, 59.
6. Georg G. Iggers, *Historiography in the Twentieth Century: From Scientific Objectivity to the Postmodern Challenge* (Hanover, CT: Wesleyan University Press, 1997), 9–10.
7. Quoted in Iggers, *Historiography in the Twentieth Century*, 10.
8. Quoted in Iggers, *Historiography in the Twentieth Century*, 12.

# Index

Acton, Lord, 4
Adams, Henry, 42
Adams, Herbert Baxter, 111, 112
Alexander, Ruth M., 125
Alperovitz, Gar, 133
Andrews, Charles McLean, 111
Annales/Annaliste school,
116–117
Appleby, Joyce, 125
Ariès, Philippe, 117
Aristotle, 80
Assyrians, 5, 13–14
Augustine, St., 21–22, 32, 37, 51, 69
Aydelotte, William O., 120

Bacon, Francis, 71
Bancroft, George, 41, 45, 111
Barnes, Robert, 31
Barthes, Roland, 134
Barzun, Jacques, 122
Beard, Charles Austin, 84,
112–113, 114
Becker, Carl L., 83, 113, 114
Bede, Venerable, 24
Beer, George Louis, 111
Beezley, W. H. T., 117
Bender, Thomas, 125
Benson, Lee, 119
Berkhofer, Robert, 135
Berlin, Isaiah, 85–86
Bernstein, Barton, 133
Blassingame, John W., 123–124
Bloch, Marc, 33, 116
Bodin, Jean, 33
Book reviews, 90–91
Boorstin, Daniel, 119
Boronius, Caesar, 32
Bossuet, Jacques Bénigne, 33
Bradford, William, 34
Braudel, Fernand, 117
Breisach, Ernst, 108, 116
Brodie, Fawn M., 121
Buckle, Henry Thomas, 73
Bullitt, William C., 121
Bury, J. B., 109

Caesar, Julius, 18–19
Camden, William, 34
Cause, problem with term, 80–81
Chartier, Roger, 135

Christian historical consciousness,
12, 19–26
Cliometrics, 119–120
Collingwood, Robin G., 7, 34,
35–36, 38, 42, 75, 76–78
Comte, Auguste, 73–75
Condorcet, Marie Jean Antoine, 54
Conkin, Paul K., 4, 84
Coulanges, Fustel de, 110
Covering–law model, 79–80, 81
Croce, Benedetto, 75–76, 114–115
Cyclical view, 51, 59–60

Dependency theory, 59
Derrida, Jacques, 134
Descartes, René, 1, 32, 38–39, 71
Dialectical materialism, 56
Dialectic approach to history,
43–44, 56
Dilthey, Wilhelm, 75
Doctoral dissertations, 88–89
Donald, David H., 121
Dray, William, 79, 80
Du Bois, W. E. B., 114
Dunning, William A., 113

Ego, 64, 65
Eliade, Mircea, 51
Eliot, Samuel, 113
Elton, G. R., 72–73
Engels, Friedrich, 55–56
Engerman, Stanley L., 120
Enlightenment, 34–40
Erikson, Erik H., 121
Eusebius of Caesarea, 20–21

Febvre, Lucien, 116
Fogel, Robert William, 72–73,
119–120
Ford, Henry, 1
Foucault, Michel, 134
Frankfurt school, 115
Freud, Sigmund, 58, 64–67, 121
Froissart, Jean, 25
Fromm, Erich, 115
Fukuyama, Francis, 2

Gardner, Lloyd C., 123
Gay, Peter, 122
Genovese, Eugene D., 124